Safe Kids, Safe Families

Samantha Wilson

Safe Kids, Safe Families

C Collins

Safe Kids, Safe Families

© 2005 by Samantha Wilson. All rights reserved.

First published in hardcover by Collins, an imprint of HarperCollins Publishers Ltd: 2005.
This trade paperback edition: 2006.

Kidproof Canada™ is a trademark.

HarperCollins books may be purchased for educational, business, or sales promotional use through our Special Markets Department.

HarperCollins Publishers Ltd
2 Bloor Street East, 20th Floor
Toronto, Ontario, Canada
M4W 1A8

www.harpercollins.ca

Library and Archives Canada Cataloguing in Publication

Wilson, Samantha, 1966-
Safe kids, safe families : strategies for keeping your family safe at home, at school and on the Internet / Samantha Wilson. –1st trade pbk. ed.
Includes index.

ISBN-13: 978-0-00-639518-8
ISBN-10: 0-00-639518-X

1. Children–Crimes against–Prevention.
2. Teenagers–Crimes against–Prevention.
3. Safety education. 4. Child rearing. I. Title.

HQ769.W782 2006   649'.1   C2006-902433-2

RRD 9 8 7 6 5 4 3 2 1

Printed and bound in the United States
Set in Monotype Plantin and Bell Gothic

This is for my dad

If only heaven would give you back for just a day—
to hear you say one last time, "Oh, Jodi!"

I will love you forever and miss you eternally.

Contents

Introduction

What Does It Mean to Be a "Safe Family"?

When I became a parent, I was not yet a cop. When I became a cop, I was not yet a child safety advocate—or so I thought. When I became a child safety advocate, I realized that I had been one all along. I became one from the moment I held my first-born son in my arms.

There are no words to describe the feelings and emotions I felt then. I can only attempt to explain that it was like a burst of sudden pride, amazement, confusion, fear, and unconditional love that completely and utterly engulfed me.

In the beginning, I chose a parenting style that many of my friends would describe as "over-the-top protective." I felt such an overwhelming need to protect my son that I would rarely let others (even family) hold him, for fear they would drop him. I spent hours watching him in amazement. I could hear his softest cries long before anyone else could. I could predict when he was going to be fussy, upset, or uncomfortable. If he cried, I ran to his side.

I wanted so much for my son to be safe, and I had to be sure I was doing everything I could to ensure it. So I began to learn about my community, the risks my son might face one day, and what I could do to protect him. And I read a lot. But, seventeen years ago, most books on parenting were rather boring, and often less than practical: they did not address child safety beyond advising parents to cover their electrical outlets and keep things out of baby's reach. I attended seminars and watched every television program about kids and safety I could find, though they were few and far between.

I was fascinated with personal safety and the power of proactive, preventive approaches. It didn't take long before I knew that what I needed to be was a cop.

As a parent, I looked inward at my family and children and concentrated on their safety alone. As a police officer, I chose to extend my concern for the safety of all people and children within my community. I had many roles to play. I was a teacher, advisor, listener, mediator, counselor, and referee. I learned, through the experiences and tragedies of others, that there is a lot more we can do to protect our children. Too often, I heard heartbreaking comments like these from parents:

How could this happen? I knew him well, or at least I thought I did. He seemed like such a nice guy . . .

My child is very smart, and I have gone over the rules with him so many times. He knows not to talk to strangers. But he is so friendly. I told him not to be. He didn't listen. Why didn't he listen?

I know his friends — well, most of them. I know his teacher. He has been going to that school since he was in kindergarten. Why weren't they watching him?

I keep the computer in the living room so I can see my daughter when she is online. I don't understand all the stuff that she does on it, but she told me not to worry so much. I had no idea . . . How could I have?

She said she was just going over to a friend's house. That was three days ago. I didn't ask who her friend was. I didn't think it was any of my business. After all, she is seventeen.

She seemed like such a great lady. She had two kids of her own. The house was clean, and she was so nice. She even gave me references. I don't understand how she could have done this to my child.

Seeing and hearing so much confusion over how to be a *safe family*, I realized that what parents needed was clear direction, and a positive, proactive focus on child safety.

Introduction

Safe families are empowered by knowledge, not disabled by fear. They do not choose to ignore or deny potential danger; instead, they learn everything they can about it. Knowledge is empowering. The more you know about how something happened, what went wrong, and how it could have been prevented, the better prepared you will be.

As a police officer and a child safety expert, I have met many parents who live in constant fear for the safety of their kids, fear that affects every decision they make. They are consumed with the horror they see daily in the media, and are driven to protect their kids at any cost. I applaud their devotion. However, too much fear can often disguise the warning signs of dangerous people and situations, and actually cause you to make unsafe choices. *If you allow yourself to become consumed with fear you will not be able to protect your kids.*

The only thing you need to fear is what you do not understand or know about, because if you can see the dangers, and understand the threats that your kids face, you can prepare for them. If you don't look at them, they will sneak up behind you, and you will be left with the reactive response, which you might say is like crossing your fingers and hoping for the best.

Let's face it, there are terrible tragedies reported every day in the media, some with details that I truly believe only the police and other professionals need to know. The safe parent has to learn about these dangers, but they won't focus on the gruesome details. They'll gain insight by finding the point in the story where a *choice* changed the course of events.

A safe parent is able to predict when good will go bad as easily as knowing when their child is in need. Being able to predict when good will go bad is about "tickling" your natural ability to recognize the warning signals sent by people, places, and things. A safe parent is someone who is able to separate perceived danger from the real thing, someone who is able to predict danger and prevent tragedy. That parent is you.

* * *

Even though it has been four years since I left policing to devote all my time to Kidproof, there is still a large part of me that thinks and reacts like a cop. I look at people, situations, and events a little differently than most people might. I look beyond the crime itself and into the events and situations that led up to it. I look at their future implications rather than focus on their present. I guess it will always be that way, and to me it feels like a gift rather than a burden.

But you don't need to be a cop, or encounter the same experiences that I did, to keep your own kids safe. There are always warning signs. You just need to know what to look for, be willing to accept the truth of your own instincts, and have the courage to act on what you know.

Understand that you have the ability to protect your kids. Be confident in that.

Safe kids have safe parents, and safe families. It may sound simple, but it's also true: crimes can be prevented, violence is predictable, and knowledge is the key.

Chapter One

Protecting Kids:
Whose Job Is It Anyway?

My heart still misses a beat when I think about a family I met while I was a police officer. In fact, I can feel my chest tighten as I tell the story to you.

It was six o'clock in the evening and still light outside as I took a police report from a woman whose eight-year-old son had been missing for three hours.

"I have street-proofed my son," said the woman. "He knows not to talk to strangers."

The child's disappearance was alarming enough, but the mother's reaction shocked me: I realized that some parents actually think their children can protect themselves.

The woman lived in a nice neighborhood in London, Ontario, the sort of neighborhood that most people, passing through, might consider living in. She was well educated, had a good job, and, judging from the books that were displayed in her den, liked to read. She had two children: a ten-year-old girl and the missing eight-year-old boy.

I noticed a women's magazine on the kitchen counter, with a shoutline that read, "Top Ten Spring Projects to Do with Your Kids." A portrait of the woman and her two children was displayed on the wall. The house was clean, and there were neat rows of kids' shoes by the back door.

Missing children reports were not uncommon, but this mother's complete lack of concern caught me off guard. She explained that she was certain her son would never talk to strangers or do anything dangerous.

She had actually waited several hours before she called the police, and even then, her actions seemed obligatory at best. She truly believed that her son had the tools and skills he needed to protect himself.

As both a mother and a police officer, I felt differently.

You see, she wasn't necessarily a bad parent. She was just a parent who was not properly informed. She believed that her children were able to protect themselves. She thought all she needed to do was talk to them about the standard child safety issues, such as what would happen if they were abducted, talked to strangers, did drugs, smoked cigarettes, or hung out with the wrong crowd. She made sure to pepper each lesson with frightening examples of the horrible things that could happen to them. Then, miraculously—poof—her kids would be safe!

I had just started collecting the information I needed to begin the search for this little boy when he burst through the front door and threw his coat onto a chair. He stopped hard in front of me. In full uniform, I must have seemed like a giant.

"Where were you?" the woman asked her son, somewhat embarrassed.

"Outside, playing in a fort in the bush," he answered, almost surprised at the question.

The woman quickly apologized for bothering the police, and said that she no longer needed me. I walked over and looked closely at the little boy, who was very small but had huge, innocent eyes. I couldn't help smiling.

"Actually," I said, "you do."

....

I wanted to share this story with you for two reasons. First, like many stories of children who go missing for brief periods of time, it has a happy ending.

Second, it illustrates the most common threat to your child's safety, a threat that outweighs that of the pedophile, predator, drug dealer, bully, and every other thug on the street. The threat I'm talking about is this: shifting the responsibility of protecting kids *onto the kids themselves*.

The responsibility of child safety belongs to everyone. This includes you, me, your neighbors, schools, educators, police, and politicians. Kids themselves should be considered the very last line of defense. Yet all too often children are left to protect themselves.

Of course, I am a hard and fast supporter of child safety education, but there is no such thing as a program that will ultimately keep your kids safe. There is no magic cloak that will shield them from harm and no perfect rule that will never be broken. You see, kids need to learn how to make safe choices, but they need you to reinforce, support, and encourage them from the beginning.

Safe Parents, Safe Kids

I have no clue what *you* might have been told as a child, or what you might have picked up since you became a parent. Many parents continue to use old tactics that simply don't work in today's world. To be on the safe side, let's start fresh. In the chapters to come, I will cover numerous topics in detail, but for now I want to mention the basics of safe kids and safe families.

The bottom line is that *safe kids have safe parents*. What are the traits of safe parents?

- They provide suitable layers of protection for their children.
- They can distinguish between real and perceived danger.
- They pay attention to situations and details more than places.
- They question the motives of people who come in contact with their family.
- They are aware of the new ways predators lure kids away.
- They recognize their limitations and accept that it takes an entire community to keep their kids safe.

Layers of Protection

When you think about protecting your kids, you need to consider it in terms of "layering." Layering is based on the premise that there is no single tool that is magical, foolproof, criminal-proof and will always keep you safe. When you apply several layers of protection, you increase your chances of success: if one layer fails, the next kicks in.

However, each layer is as important as the next. There is no point in taking the time and effort to add a layer of protection if it is easily defeated. Invest equal amounts of time and energy into each layer, and remember that your child is the first but most vulnerable layer of defense. Prepare for your plan to fail and always have a backup.

As an example of layering, let's look at how you can protect your child from drowning if you have a swimming pool.

First, identify the hazard—the swimming pool.

Next, identify the minimum level of protection—your child.

Now apply layers of protection around your child.

Layer 1 – Your child

Invest in quality swimming instruction and preventive safety education. Teach your child to swim, and about the rules for playing in and around the swimming pool. Keep the pool off-limits to your child except when you or another responsible adult are there to supervise.

Layer 2 – Wrist alarm

Have your child wear a wrist swimming pool alarm. This is an alarm that looks similar to a watch. If the wrist alarm gets wet because the child has waded or fallen into water, the receiver will sound.

Layer 3 – Swimming pool alarm

Install an alarm in your pool that will sound if there is any movement or disturbance to the water.

Layer 4 – Physical barriers

Prevent access to the swimming pool by building a fence around the pool. Ensure that the fence has a secure gate, with a self-closing latch.

Layer 5 – Gate and door alarms

If your child is able to open the gate, have an alarm set to alert you that the gate has been opened. Place a door alarm on all doors to the house that lead to the swimming pool area.

If a door is opened, you will be advised.

Layer 6 – Supervise, supervise, supervise

There is no better way to protect your children than to supervise them. Nothing replaces supervision.

The process of layering used in this example is a good model for protecting your child from any hazard. The ultimate level of protection is always the same: YOU.

To be sure that you are applying the correct layers of protection, you will need to follow some simple guidelines.

1. Learn about the potential threats.
2. Start with the minimum level of protection.
3. Build from that level.
4. Complete the process with parental or adult supervision.

Danger—Real or Not?

From the moment that your child was born, he was given a special gift, a power that can help to keep him safe throughout his life. This power is called *instinct*.

How do kids know when their instincts are warning them that something is not right? They might feel "butterflies," an upset stomach, sweaty hands, or a pounding heart. They might describe the feeling they have as uncomfortable or nervous, or maybe they'll just say that someone seems "creepy." Adults may call it intuition, a gut feeling, a personal alarm, or a premonition. It really doesn't matter how it is articulated, what matters is that it is validated.

I like to think of instinct as the "Spidy-sense" that the superhero Spider-Man had. In fact, that is how I explain it to my kids. Do you remember Peter Parker? Of course, he *is* Spider-Man, and along

ı, speed, and grip, he has a keen ability to
sistent itching at the base of his skull that tells
by. This sense is so powerful that he can zone
ger with the accuracy of radar. It works for all
t those that are potentially life-threatening. It
f switch, and it is not learned. It just is—and
of the time.

Man is just a comic book superhero, and his
d fictional, but they are not as different from
 think.

eaning that you are born with it. It is not
 forget it. However, you can certainly sup-
se to listen to it. Many people do, and often
 too late, "I knew something felt wrong . . ."
ng keep you—and your kids—safe? Here's
nstinct as several different types of alarms.
ered by situations and feelings. Each alarm
nd appropriate response. Let me give you

Routine Response

ıs set our alarm clocks before we go to bed.
und and wake us when we need to get up.
s alarm are routine, and don't take much
d of the alarm triggers you to act a certain
, that includes dragging yourself out of bed
r the coffee! Your alarm clock triggered your

ore Response

e mall, and as you are walking away you hear
 the area of your car. You glance over to be
ut once you realize it isn't, and that there
one breaking into another car, you determine
ou. So you move on without giving it much

more attention. This alarm caused you to momentarily pay closer attention to the situation, but after a quick assessment, you realized that you did not need to do anything about it. This alarm triggered your ignore response.

Fire alarm equals your Action Response

You have taken your kids to a movie and the theater is packed. Just before the movie starts, the fire alarm sounds. You notice a strong odor of smoke. You realize that there is likely a fire and take control of the situation, gather your family, and quickly exit the building. It was obvious to you, based on the sound of the fire alarm, and the additional smell of smoke, that there was a fire. You needed to take action to stay safe and protect your family. These indicators caused you to react immediately and triggered your action response.

Each of these alarms caused you to react differently, either out of routine, annoyance, or emergency. The mere presence of them told you what to do. There was no need to question what they meant. Your responses were based on past experiences and training over the years. The alarm itself was merely a trigger for an appropriate and *learned* safe response. You didn't hear the fire alarm, smell the smoke, and then say, "I have no idea what that is but it sure is annoying. I am just going to ignore it." Instead, you responded appropriately based on a trigger—*the alarm.*

If instinct is your child's personal alarm, his feelings are its trigger. When bad feelings are present, his personal alarm will sound, triggering him to respond safely.

In order for your kids to trust and rely on their instincts to keep them safe you need to do two things: validate their instincts; and role-play safe and appropriate responses to their feelings.

Validate their instincts

If your children do not trust their instincts, and are not listening to their feelings, they will be vulnerable and at risk. Do not allow feelings like embarrassment, fear, and lack of confidence turn an action response into an ignore response. Adults do it all the time, and what's worse is that, without even knowing it, they often teach kids to do the same. This can be potentially disastrous and leave your child unprotected. However, you can ensure this does not happen by validating their instincts from the time they are infants.

Here is a great example of how easy it is to dismiss your child's feelings when they are triggered by her personal alarms and instincts.

As a new parent, you want to show off your beautiful baby to the world. After all, she is so amazing and it is hard to believe that you created such a perfect little girl! People are always asking to hold her, and being the proud parent, you are happy to oblige.

However, not all babies love to be held by everyone who asks. Simply being placed in an unknown person's arms may cause them to squirm, scream, wail, and do whatever else is necessary to convince you that they are feeling uncomfortable.

Now, here is the part that even I have been guilty of. You place your new bundle of joy into someone's arms and she completely freaks out. It is obvious that she is not comfortable. Instead of validating her feelings and responses by taking her from the person, you feel embarrassed and you politely try to explain that she is just a bit fussy. You may even tell the person holding her to walk with her, or give her a soother—anything to stop the crying.

Pretty soon, you give up and take your screaming bundle of joy back into your arms and she abruptly stops crying. Had she screamed because she didn't like the person, did she sense something was wrong, or was she just trying to make you understand what she needed? Maybe she just wanted to feel safe, and needed you to respond to her feelings. It doesn't mean that the person who was holding her is dangerous—it simply means that your child did not want to be with him or her.

Babies have not developed sophisticated responses to their feelings, nor have they learned to ignore their personal alarms. In fact, a baby's instincts are as pure and in tune as they can possibly be. Your child has fully developed instincts from the moment she is born. She may not be able to tell you in words how she feels but she will alert you to the fact that she is "feeling" something.

You listen to your baby's cries for food, sleep, or a clean diaper; now just expand your understanding of what makes her uncomfortable to include people. Don't worry if your children are no longer infants; it is not too late. Start immediately. Resist the temptation to dismiss your child's feelings by explaining that he may just be tired, or acting silly. By dismissing or minimizing children's intuitive communication, you will only teach them to dismiss their feelings later in life. And it is later in life, when you are not by their side, that they will need it most.

Role-play safe and appropriate responses to their feelings

You don't need to experience something to know how to respond safely to it. As the saying goes, "You don't need to be hit with a stick to know it hurts!" It is absurd to think that children need to be victimized to learn how to react safely. Role-play and practice scenarios will teach them how to avoid dangerous situations.

Children often practice fire drills at school. This is done for a reason. Routine practice plays a significant role in the successful outcome of an actual emergency. If people have rehearsed safe responses to a trigger (alarm) they will likely revert to them automatically when they need to. In a dangerous situation, there is seldom time to think: you must simply react. The chances of your children reacting safely are far greater if they trust their instincts *and* have been taught how to respond.

Here's how to conduct a role-playing exercise.

Think of a situation that you feel could be potentially dangerous for your child. Describe the situation to him in detail, making it realistic but not threatening or scary. You do not need to use scare tactics to teach your child to stay safe.

Ask him to identify a feeling he might have in that situation, and then to identify what is causing the feeling. Ask him what he thinks would be a safe response to the situation and feeling, and discuss his answers.

Ask him what he would want the outcome to be. Discuss the

scenario until there is a positive and successful outcome. Review the situation, feeling, and response. Don't be afraid to offer him suggestions. This exercise is not a test, but it will give you some valuable insight as to how your child responds to certain situations. Don't be alarmed if he has nothing to say. Remember, he may not have experienced such a situation yet, and naturally will have nothing to draw from. This is the whole reason for the role-play—now he does!

You Have the Power

Here it is, plain, simple, and to the point. You have more control over your child's safety than you may feel. Often it is those around you that make you feel vulnerable and powerless when it comes to your children and their safety. Conflicting advice, media hype, and mixed messages all contribute to your questioning your abilities, and your fear of the outside world. You need to be confident that you have the power to protect your children right now, and give them the skills they need to continue to make safe choices throughout their lives.

I am going to share something with you that will help you make the right choice any time you are faced with a decision about your child's safety.

Violence is predictable. Common sense tells us that if something can be predicted, we can prepare for it, and ultimately prevent it from happening. *But you have to open your eyes to see it coming—and then take control of the situation.* Crossing your fingers, following old tactics, and hoping for the best are not the answer.

Control means that you, the parent, choose the degree of risk in a given situation. The higher the risk taken, the greater and more severe the consequences could be. Children are not yet capable of making decisions related to risks. That is your job. Your choices will determine how safe your children will be when they are young, and will teach them safe responses as they grow older and more independent.

For example, if you choose to leave your baby in your car while you quickly run into the corner store, you are obviously increasing the risk of your child becoming distressed, overheated or cold, or, worst of all, abducted. You are in control of the situation, but your choices have actually increased the risk of danger.

If you choose to take your baby with you, even though it is difficult and time-consuming, you have also controlled the situation, but you have decreased the risk of danger. You have exercised complete control at all times. The choice about how much risk you were willing to take was yours.

It is important to note, however, that although by making a safe choice you have reduced the risk, you cannot and will not be able to remove it entirely.

Risk is part of everything we do. There is a risk that you will burn your cake if you do not time it properly; there is a risk that you will not feel well tomorrow if you stay out late tonight; there is a risk that your children will become injured if you do not supervise them; there is a risk to your family's safety if you do not protect them.

You have control only over your own behavior and surroundings. Period. You cannot control what someone else may do, or how other parents safeguard their children. You can't control when a predator decides to strike, but you can control the access they have to your kids.

Parents are faced with constant and simultaneous choices from the moment that their child is born. Some choices are more obvious, such as not leaving your child unattended in a car, and others are cleverly disguised.

Tracy, a friend of mine, has a lovely daughter named Chelsea, who is in grade one. This little girl is very sociable, outgoing and quite a character. Her mom is cautious, sets boundaries, sticks to punishments, and enforces rules. She is conscientious but not paranoid. She is like the majority of parents I meet, and her story is also hauntingly common.

Tracy runs a hair salon out of her home. She is usually very busy with work, home life, social engagements, and planning her children's activities.

Tracy has an arrangement with a neighbor, who also has a child in grade one, to pick up Chelsea after school. This way, Tracy can fit in a few more clients before the end of the day.

One very hectic day in the salon, Tracy received a phone call from her neighbor around the time that school was being dismissed. The neighbor told her that Chelsea had been invited to go over to the house of another child in her class and she desperately wanted to go.

Instinctively, Tracy said no. She did not know the mother of the other child, and did not feel that Chelsea should go. But that answer was not very popular with Chelsea. She began to scream and cry and beg her mom to let her go to the other girl's home.

Tracy stood her ground in a heated discussion with her six-year-old, all the while juggling the phone, a pair of scissors, and waiting customers.

She told Chelsea that she did not know the other mommy, did not know where she lived, and that they would have to arrange for another time to visit and play. But Chelsea was having no part of reason. She simply wanted to go.

An argument ensued, and Tracy became increasingly angry and frustrated. Finally, the other girl's mother took the phone from Chelsea and spoke to Tracy. It was obvious that this woman was very offended at Tracy's reaction and began to argue and state that she was a good mother and would obviously take care of Chelsea. Of course, all this was done while Chelsea listened in.

Tracy began to give in to the stress, confusion, and bullying from both her daughter and the woman. Against her better judgment, she finally agreed to allow Chelsea to go to the woman's home but requested that the woman call her as soon as she arrived home. Tracy intended to pick up Chelsea soon after.

The woman agreed and hung up. Tracy was upset by the confrontation with her daughter and the woman, but mostly because she had given in to them. She realized that in her confusion she had neglected to ask for the woman's phone number, or to find out where she lived.

With no idea where Chelsea was going, Tracy could only hope that the woman would call her soon. Over an hour passed, and still there was no phone call.

Tracy began to panic. She called around to other parents and eventually found the name and address of the woman who had taken Chelsea to her home. She lived close to one of Tracy's good friends.

Tracy still had clients in her salon and felt that she could not get away, so she called her friend and asked her to go and pick up Chelsea. When the friend arrived, Chelsea was playing happily with her new friend. The mother easily let this stranger, who was obviously not Chelsea's mother, take Chelsea away. The woman never did call Tracy.

Fortunately, this story did not have a tragic outcome. Tracy and Chelsea were very lucky. And while it's easy to point fingers at any one of these individuals and place blame, it is more important to identify the turning points—and there were many—and the factors that influenced Tracy's decisions.

As a parent reading this story, you may recall being in a similar situation in which your instincts told you to do one thing but time, convenience, fear of confrontation or embarrassment compelled you to do another. Let's look at how those factors can lead to unsafe choices, and how you can overcome them.

Reasons vs. Excuses

You, as a parent, have control over your child's safety. You always have. And your children, contrary to media hype, are not sitting ducks. That's the good news.

The bad news is that parents often make decisions that can affect the safety of their children for ill-conceived and frivolous reasons.

Most parents, not unlike Tracy, will look for reasons to justify their decisions to go against their instincts. Many believe that a feeling is not enough, that they should have proof of someone or something being potentially dangerous. But each situation will give you advance warning signals that are crystal clear, signals that are all the proof you need to follow your instincts and make the safe choice. You have to be willing to look for and see them, and not allow other factors to interfere and make the decision for you.

Bad choices are usually based on poor excuses:

Excuse one: **Embarrassment**
Excuse two: **Avoidance**
Excuse three: **Ignorance**
Excuse four: **Convenience**

Embarrassment

Parents are often concerned about how they appear to other parents, teachers, their boss, or even their kids. Many will do almost anything to avoid an embarrassing situation. To make decisions without being influenced by embarrassment, force yourself to look at the embarrassing moment as just that—a moment that will pass. Don't allow the moment to be the turning point where good goes to bad.

Avoidance

Sometimes it seems easiest to just agree to do something to avoid confrontation. After all, some people can be so insistent! A clear warning sign that someone is trying to control you is when they won't take no for an answer. Every parent knows how difficult it can be to stick to your no, especially when your kids want something. But the bottom line is that if you are around, you make the decisions about your children's safety, *not them*. I know it is hard and kids can be demanding, but stick to your no and move on. You can avoid danger if you learn *not* to avoid confrontation.

Ignorance

Not my favorite word, but *ignorance* is the best word to describe the "nothing bad could ever happen to us" attitude. Anything can happen. It is your job as a parent to control the risk associated with every situation your child faces. You need to invest the time to learn

the hazards, weigh the risks, and go into ea
realistic view of your child's risks. Believing
reserved for the teenagers of the world, not

Convenience

Let's face it. Once you have a baby, convenie
movement are out the nursery door! I am
have been for both my sons' lives. I unders
life, married life, and parenthood. I get it. I
fight it.

Convenience is one of the most comme
unsafe choices. "I'm late for dinner so I'll j
we tell ourselves. Or "The baby is asleep in
into the store without him and lock the car c
minute." We have all felt the lure of raising
ience. In fact, we are all likely guilty of at lea

It can take only seconds for good to go b
fool you: time is not always on your side.

In a seminar with a group of parents, I u
and Chelsea to illustrate the difference
excuses. Below is a list of how the parents in
uation, and the factors that influenced T
Chelsea go to the friend's house. See if you c
and the excuses.

- Tracy was busy and distracted with the c
  not think straight.
- Chelsea was yelling at her and would not
  answer.
- The woman had a daughter who was als
  For that reason she could be trusted.
- Tracy felt bad for making the woman thi
  judging her to be a bad parent.
- It was easier to let Chelsea go and pick h
  to continue with the battle.

- Tracy was angry at the scene Chelsea was making and felt embarrassed for her neighbor, who was doing her a favor in the first place.
- Tracy trusted the woman would call her.

I asked the parents if Tracy had any control over each decision she'd made. The answers were clearly yes. However, she made choices based on excuses rather than safe reasons.

When you make a decision that involves the safety of your child, you need to test your reasoning. Is your decision being made to reduce risk—or is it an excuse? Excuses give you permission to go against your instincts, but they will enhance rather than eliminate the risk.

Facing the Risks

The world is different than it was when we were kids. New threats such as the Internet have made predators more mobile and anonymous than in the past. Meanwhile, the increased number of latchkey kids, and the growing gang and drug violence that infiltrate suburbs, give parents plenty of reasons to be concerned.

But in your quest for your children's safety, a quest that requires unremitting effort and diligence, you are not alone. And you do not have to send your kids into the world without protection. There may not be a science to keeping kids safe, but there are basic principles and skills you can learn that will guide you in any situation. If you can look at the dangers head-on, recognize the warning signs, and make safe choices, you will have safe kids and a safe family. Keep reading to find out how.

Chapter Two

Out with the Old, in with the New: Today's Rules for Keeping Your Kids Safe

When I was a kid, my parents never even thought about crime and nothing bad happened to me. Besides, I can hardly stand to think about anything happening to my kids! Maybe I should just be as careful as I know how, and hope for the best?

There are some things I miss from my childhood: more potato chips in a Hostess bag, wishing for snow in the winter, and believing that nothing really bad *could* ever happen.

On the other hand, as an adult I know that too many potato chips are fattening, snow in the winter seems to last forever, and nothing really bad *should* ever happen—but sometimes it does.

It may seem that your childhood was free from the fear of crime and violence, but it likely wasn't. Most often, it was simply not discussed. But don't think for a minute that your parents did not worry for your safety the same way you do for your own kids'.

I think of how vulnerable previous generations must have felt without the advice and guidance that parents have access to today. They got only tidbits of horror stories such as the Lindbergh baby kidnapping or Patty Hearst. And they knew, sometimes at first hand, about sexual and physical abuse, bullying, and neglect. It happened then, as it happens now.

But the good news is that as a parent today, you are better armed to protect yourself and your families than your parents could ever have dreamed of. Information-sharing among police, experts, advocates, and communities makes our job of parenting much easier, and ensures our kids have a much safer future.

Information also has to be shared in another direction: with our kids themselves. In this chapter, I'll lead you through some of the most important safety messages for you and your children to know. But first I want to address the issue of *how to talk to your kids about safety*. You probably already know how important it is to talk with them about their everyday lives and their fantastic, exciting accomplishments. But you also need to discuss the potential dangers they may face, their not-so-great decisions, and the risky choices they may make.

Children will look to their parents for guidance. You know you are neither immortal nor fearless, and so should your children. They need to be able to understand your concerns in order to believe that your concerns are real—and could actually happen. Until your children can accept that they are not invincible, they will never be truly safe.

This doesn't mean you should scare them by talking about horrific, traumatic events and telling them that "this could happen to you too." Making your kids fearful is the worst thing you can do. You want to empower them with knowledge and confidence.

Talk about real issues, real concerns, and potential risks. Do not conjure up an unlikely event to illustrate your point. If you use unusual and dramatic stories as examples, your child will only focus on preparing for the same type of unusual circumstances—which are unlikely to repeat themselves exactly. Use common, everyday situations as your examples because it is most often normal situations, not freak accidents, that go bad. These pose the greatest risk to your kids.

And don't be afraid to talk about *their* concerns as well as yours. You may find that they are most fearful of something that is very unlikely to happen. Ask them to explain what it is about the situation that scares them most. Try to narrow it down to one or two specific issues. Discuss each issue in detail, without focusing on the horror of an event they might have heard of. Instead, talk with your child about finding a time in each event when a choice was presented. Discuss what would be a safe and unsafe choice, and look at what the child involved did right and what he or she did wrong. Then move on. Working through their fears in this way will give them knowledge that empowers rather than paralyzes.

Talking about safety with your kids does not have to be something you dread, or even something you plan. Any time you see an opportunity to talk to them about safety, take it! If you see a child who wanders away from his mother in a mall, point it out and talk about it. If you read a story about a child who ran away after being approached by a stranger, point it out and talk about it. Talk, talk, talk.

Times may have changed, but some truths about good parenting haven't. It's still true, and will always be true, that keeping the lines of communication open—which is another way to describe talking!—is one of the most powerful tools you have as a parent. If your kids know they can talk to you about anything, they will talk to you when they first get a bad feeling, not after—when it will be too late.

Still, in a changing and often violent world, it's important to re-examine the safety rules and tactics that parents live by. Today, parents need to make a commitment to relearn proper safety skills, rethink their current safety plans, and reassess their environment. Yes, that is a lot of redoing—but it's necessary.

From this moment, toss out everything you have ever learned about keeping kids safe. Why? You see, child safety has been a concern for a very long time. Over the years, some experts, and some pseudo-experts, have developed or concocted strategies and technological inventions in hopes of protecting kids. But the fact is that most of them simply don't work. In this chapter, we'll look at what doesn't work any longer, and what does.

"Don't Talk to Strangers"

If you are like other parents, grandparents, teachers, or anyone else who has spoken to children about safety, I am certain you have uttered the words "Don't talk to strangers."

In the past, we believed that by teaching children not to talk to strangers, we were protecting them from abduction, abuse, and crime. But we know now it's not as simple as that.

Who is a stranger anyway? Your definition and your child's may be quite different. You may think of a stranger as someone you don't know, have not spoken to, or have never met. Your child, on the other hand, may view strangers as people she has never *seen*. She may see your neighbor every day out in his yard, and may even wave to him as she passes by. Your child probably does not view your neighbor as a stranger when, in fact, he is.

Too often, when using "stranger" in the context of child safety, we (and especially our children) imagine a dirty, creepy man who is evil to the bone. The irony is that some men who are dirty are just homeless or sick, and not necessarily dangerous. Likewise, some truly dangerous people look "normal" and harmless. And, of course, just because someone is a stranger does not mean he or she is dangerous.

Strangers have been the focus of parents' worst fears for years. Yet the truth is that crimes against kids are almost always committed by someone who is not a stranger at all. Offenders usually have had some previous contact with the family or child. Most often, they are closer than you think.

We continue to regard strangers as the enemy because one of the cornerstones of our closest relationships is trust—and we do not expect to be harmed by those we trust. As well, although the thought of anyone harming our children is excruciating, it's more painful to think of our sons or daughters being hurt by someone we know, trust, and even love. It is much easier to look outward, to a stranger, than inward to neighbors, friends, and family.

What are the repercussions of teaching children to fear strangers? What happens, for instance, when a child who has been told not to talk to strangers becomes lost? Who is he going to ask for help if he's terrified and unsure of everyone? He is going to go with anyone who does not resemble a creepy, scary stranger. But because predators come guised in many different ways—and are usually quite approachable—a scared and desperate child is the perfect target.

Rather than teaching children not to talk to strangers, you want to teach them that not all strangers are bad, and that there are far more people who will help them than hurt them. Unlike the scared child, who unwittingly waits for the predator to choose him, the confident child trusts his instincts about what makes him feel comfortable and will select a safer person.

But how do we teach children that some people are not as they appear? How do we help them determine who is safe and who is not?

We can't expect children to be able to assess someone's capacity for violence in a matter of moments; we would be fools to believe this is possible, even for an adult. Unless someone does something alarming or obviously threatening or dangerous, you will not be able to tell if he or she is a safe person, so don't fool your kids into thinking they can.

What you need to do is empower your children with self-confidence and trust in their ability to sense when something is just not right. It doesn't matter whether they can articulate it; they just have to feel it. And the best way to learn about someone, even in a very short time, is by talking.

Talking will not put your children in danger. Talking will actually increase their awareness and give them clues about whether the person they are talking with is safe. It is actually good for your kids to talk to strangers. In fact, they do it all the time, such as when you encourage them to say hello to someone they have just met but do not know.

What puts your child in danger is *going with a predator*. Willingly getting into a car, a house, or walking away without asking permission from you, the parent, is how most children end up in dangerous situations. When a predator begins to talk to your child, he too is making an assessment: of your child's vulnerability. Predators are masters at communication. They easily convince children that they can be trusted. Remember, when the predator was a child, he too was taught the "don't talk to strangers" rule. He knows that most kids are thinking about this rule, so he focuses on presenting himself as someone who is not a stranger. He will be more likely to persuade your child to go with him if your child does not think he is a stranger.

Starting today, change "Don't talk to strangers" to "Never go anywhere, with anyone, without asking permission first."

This rule applies to everyone and every situation. It includes friends, family, neighbors, and of course, strangers. Parents need to know where their children are at all times. This means that if your son wants to go to the corner store a few blocks away with his friend, he has to ask first. If your daughter wants to go to her friend's house after school, she has to ask first. Every time your children walk out the door, remind them of this rule.

Code Words

Batman. Purple house. Red hat. These are all code words belonging to kids that I met while waiting outside my son's school. I didn't know these kids, and they certainly didn't know me.

These are the code words their parents have been using to supposedly protect them from being lured away by someone they don't know. Words that were to be kept secret. So how did I find out what they were? I just asked.

For those of you not familiar with the "code word" system, you are in for a treat. Years ago, there was a dilemma. It was mostly based on the fear of all strangers and the almost universal method of teaching kids not to talk to strangers. The problem was this: what would happen if you were held up in traffic and could not pick your kids up at school on time? How would you pass on permission to your kids to trust someone that you have sent for them in your place? How could you tell your kids (before the invention of cell phones) that you would be sending Uncle Charlie instead? Easy! Tell Uncle Charlie the secret code word and he in turn would tell your child. If someone knew the secret code word, they were automatically considered safe. The child then had permission to talk to them and go with them.

The code word system is so widely used that it runs the risk of

becoming as entrenched as the "don't talk to strangers" message. I
have seen it posted on safety organizations, in school newsletters,
and even on police websites. This system is not only outdated, but
potentially dangerous. Although its intentions were good, it has
serious fatal flaws.

The first and most obvious flaw is that kids can't be trusted to
keep a secret. You can live with a child's indiscretion if it means a
surprise birthday party is no longer a surprise, but a secret as
important as a code word is too risky.

I am happy to report that proponents of the code word system
also understood this flaw and came up with a solution. They suggest that you change the code word often (just in case your kids are
telling people) and always change it after it has been used.

Make sense? Not really. I can't help wondering why you would
need to change the code word after you have used it. Isn't the person you sent to collect your child trustworthy? If you feel the need
to change the word now that another person knows it, maybe that
other person wasn't a safe choice in the first place.

Besides, trying to get a child to remember a code word that
changes twice a month may be harder than you think. Quite honestly, I myself couldn't keep up!

Your child is born with strong instincts and can sense when
something is not right or someone makes him uncomfortable. A
code word should not override a child's instincts. I would never tell
my sons the following: "No matter how you are feeling, no matter
how creepy the person makes you feel, no matter if you believe him
or not, if he says the code word you should ignore every intuitive
signal you are feeling and just go with him. You have my permission." NEVER.

My sons know there would never be a time when I could not contact them, or an adult they already know and trust (like the school
principal), to tell them I would be late. I would never send a
stranger to pick them up without first telling them or the school.
This is a promise that I have made to them.

You need to promise your child the same. He does not need a

code word. He needs to trust that you will not break this promise. With the advent of cell phones and other communication tools, there is little reason for you to be cut off from notifying anyone.

Perhaps you are wondering, What happens if I am in an accident? But consider this: if you can give someone a code word to use, and the directions to where your child is, you can make the call yourself.

If your child trusts that you will never send someone to get him without telling him, and he knows never to go anywhere without asking you first, you have succeeded in reducing the risk of abduction to almost nil.

Name Tags

I have seen the oodles of mittens, jackets, pants, t-shirts, and lunch pails overflowing from lost-and-found bins at schools. I have even had the unpleasant experience of having to dig through one such bin when my son lost his "'mostest' favorite t-shirt of all time." At Kidproof Canada, we often find goodies left behind in our classes across the country. Kids forget things, lose things, and misplace things. That is predictable.

And because parents don't want to have to replace these items, and schools and camps don't want them hanging around, most people make it easy for the items to be returned: they write their child's name directly on the items.

Great idea, and it works successfully in most cases, except for my son's. That is because I don't write his name on anything. Period.

There are few things that I have absolutely no time for, and this is one of them—that's because it's a system that is convenient, but it jeopardizes the safety of kids. You may not realize it, but writing your children's names on their belongings at school or camp, or on their team jerseys is one of the most dangerous things you can do.

How can a simple thing like writing my kid's name on his lunch bag be dangerous? Here's how.

Predators are always looking for ways to convince your child that they can be trusted and, most important, that they are not strangers. They will be far more successful if they can convince your child that they have met him before. What better way than to call him by his first name?

How do they find out your child's name? Easy. All they have to do is read the bold felt-pen name written on his backpack, shoes, coat, hat, sweater, or any other belonging that is in plain view.

Your tactic to keep track of your child's belongings has suddenly turned into a tool for a predator.

But the labeling does not end at school and camp. Sports teams are notorious for sewing players' names on team jackets, sweaters, and jerseys. I have seen names on jerseys for peewee baseball up to high school soccer teams. The safety risk of labeling kids' clothing does not diminish once kids become teenagers.

With the increase of Internet use by kids and teens, predators have found new ways to contact, communicate, and gain access to their targets. I'll deal with Internet safety in more detail in chapter six, but for now let me warn you that, in spite of a growing awareness of online safety concerns, children are still giving out personal information in chat rooms and through instant messaging.

Predators have been known to physically locate their chat room "friends" by connecting small pieces of information the child has given—such as names of sport teams they play on, neighborhoods their games are held in, and arenas or fields where they might play. If a predator is determined to find his victim, and he has a name, sports team, and location, all he needs is to go to a public game and get a look at his target. If kids have their names on their jerseys, it's a snap.

I realize that replacing lost items can be costly, time-consuming, and frustrating. Short of using Super glue or changing the nature of kids, there's no way to keep them from losing things now and again. But there are safe ways to identify their belongings so you can get them back.

Have your children come up with a symbol that is unique to

them. It could be anything they like. A heart and three moons, a squiggle and a dot—whatever they choose to design.

This symbol will be used to replace their names in their belongings. Have them write, iron, fabric paint, or draw this symbol onto everything they would use in school, camp, or sports.

This is a fantastic way to label your belongings, and still keep your child's name free from outsiders' view. Of course you can use your initials, but kids much prefer to be creative. Creating this symbol also gives you an opportunity to remind your kids of one of the most important safety lessons: "Never go anywhere, with anyone, without asking permission first."

Block Parents

If children are walking in their own neighborhood and feel frightened, where can they go for help?

This is a question that most parents and safety planners have been asking for years. Let's face it. Parents can't supervise their kids and be everywhere all the time. Besides, there will come a time, usually around the age of nine or ten, when your child won't want you tagging along. They will either be walking to and from school, or playing at the local park, often without you.

The Block Parent program was developed in a response to this valid concern. It originated in London, England, during the Second World War, and it offered assistance to women, children, and the elderly in need of help. The volunteer-run program was introduced to Canadians in 1968 after a young boy was sexually assaulted and murdered in London, Ontario. The program gained momentum and began to spread across the country over the next ten years.

Although the program was initially developed to assist all members of the community, it grew to be primarily associated with protecting children. The plan was to have volunteers in each community who would be available for children if they needed help. They would display a red Block Parent sign in their front window to tell kids that theirs was a safe house to go to in need.

This program was widely promoted through safety councils, police departments, schools, and just about every other child-focused organization there was. It still is being used in some cities and communities in North America today.

Let me relate a story about my experience with the Block Parent program. When I was about ten years old, I was walking home from a friend's house with another girl. We were about a block away from my house and it was dark except for the street lights. I noticed a man walking toward us about a block away, on the same side of the street as we were. For some reason, he made me uncomfortable. He was still a distance away and I really could only see the dark outline of his body, not his face.

I moved across the street with my friend. The man crossed the street too, and continued walking toward us. I stopped and he started to walk faster. His gait was hard and determined. I knew there was something wrong. I grabbed my friend's hand and we ran up the driveway of a house that had a Block Parent sign in the window. We banged on the door. The man had now nearly reached us and he began to yell at us. Almost frantic, we continued to bang on the door for what seemed like a lifetime until finally an older man answered.

My friend quickly rattled off our story, that this man was yelling at us and we were afraid of him. The old man looked over our shoulders and asked the other man what was going on. He replied that he thought we had thrown eggs at his house and he was coming after us.

The older man, the Block Parent, told us to go home and shut the door. My friend began to cry. We were very scared and I was not sure which was worse, the old man in the house, or the angry man at the end of the driveway.

I decided to stay on the front step and yell to the angry man that it was not us who had thrown eggs at his house. My friend and I sat on the step for a few more minutes until we thought it was safe to make a mad dash for my house. Luckily, the angry man either believed me or simply gave up and went home.

I never went to a Block Parent home again.

As an adult, I can look back on that experience and realize it might have been an anomaly. I am sure there were some fantastic, committed volunteers who were proud to be Block Parents and would do anything to protect a child. Yet as a safety expert, I realize that the Block Parent program requires a little more scrutiny.

Who can be a Block Parent? If the Block Parent program is in your area, anyone can volunteer. However, in order for a family and home to be approved, they must meet the following criteria.

1. Everyone twelve years of age and over residing in the home must sign the application form, agreeing to submit to a criminal records check (through a nationally maintained crime database), and be found clear.
2. You must meet with an organizer of the Block Parent program or your local police for an interview.
3. You must supply references and agree to a background check conducted by the police.

If all of these checks are clear, you will be welcomed into the program and given the famous red sign to display in your window. You must put the Block Parent sign in your window only when you are available. Residents in a Block Parent–approved home are re-screened every two to three years, and any new resident must also be screened. According to the Block Parent Program, there has never been a reported incident where a child was harmed at a Block Parent home.

Here are the problems I see. First, the screening process does not take into account the uncle who is a pedophile who may visit the home without residing there.

Second, a Block Parent is someone you do not know and for that reason can't possibly trust. Despite the required checks, and the organization's incident-free record to date, a clear criminal record does not guarantee that someone is safe. A pedophile, for instance, has an average of thirty victims in his past before the first report is ever made to the police.

Block Parent is an old program that is outdated, unrealistic, unnecessary, and potentially dangerous for today's needs. Its premise is that *places* rather than *people* can be judged as safe—which is a dangerous error.

So where should children go if they need help? To an adult they trust because they know them, not because they have a sign that says they are safe.

When your children reach the age when they want to walk to school or play in the neighborhood on their own, it is important that you take the time to point out safe houses or businesses along the route or in the neighborhood where they can go for help. These include neighbors, shop owners, or centers that you, the parent, have decided are safe. If your child does not know the people you are pointing out, introduce them. Let these people know that you have directed your child to go to them for help if she needs it.

Self-defense

In August 2004, an eleven-year-old girl was walking down a rural road in Langley, British Columbia, with a thirteen-year-old friend. It was about 2:30 in the afternoon.

Suddenly, a mini-van swerved toward the girls, knocking the thirteen-year-old off her bicycle. The eleven-year-old was shocked and moved to help her friend. The driver jumped out of the van, grabbed the eleven-year-old girl, bound her with duct tape, and threw her into the vehicle. He drove away, leaving the thirteen-year-old on the side of the road.

The girl was driven more than twenty-five kilometers to a field, sexually assaulted, and released. (It is very rare for a predator to release his victim rather than kill her.) The girl ran to the first home she saw and asked for help.

This incident was horrific and sent a jolt of fear through this small, mainly rural community. Within days, the offender was caught because of community support, police dedication, and an abundance of leads from citizens.

Weeks later, a city councilor approached the council meeting with a proposal. She had a daughter close to the same age as the girl who had been assaulted. She proposed that self-defense lessons be taught, free of charge, to all women and children in the city. She wanted her daughter, herself, and every child to be better armed to protect themselves from this type of blitz attack.

Assaults like this are alarming, but rare, thank goodness. The reaction, however, is common. Many parents believe that self-defense is the answer to keeping kids safe. Just look in the Yellow Pages or online to see how many organizations claim to teach children to fight back.

I appeared as one of a panel of guests on a high-profile radio station to discuss child safety and how kids can protect themselves from danger. My fellow panelists were a husband-and-wife team from the United States. Like me, they both had previously been police officers, and they had recently published a book that claimed to teach kids how to protect themselves.

An important part of their safety program is to teach children to physically protect themselves by striking the perpetrator in his most vulnerable place. It is not where you think. They suggest that all children should learn to hit someone in the throat by making a V with their hands and striking with a chopping motion. They even suggest that parents encourage their children to practice on cardboard paper-towel rolls. The couple's theory is that children who practice this strike will be able, in the event of an attack, to "protect themselves."

To me this is nonsense. But the flaws in the self-defense approach to child safety are not unique to a particular book or program. There are certain assumptions and factors that are simply ignored or overlooked by self-defense advocates.

The most important factor is that when it comes to physical defense, size does matter. Most children are too small to inflict significant harm on an adult, not to mention that it is a long way up from four feet (the height of an average eight-year-old) to the throat of a six-foot-tall man. I challenge anyone to convince me that he or she could teach an eleven-year-old child weighing seventy-five pounds to defend herself against a motivated, agitated two-hundred-pound man. If he gets hold of this girl, she will only get away if he gives her the opportunity. Self-defense strategies will not protect her or anyone else.

Self-defense for personal safety is usually based on police tactical defense training, often in combination with martial arts. Techniques range from simple to complex, as do the skill levels needed to perfect them. I was trained in tactical defense as a police officer, so I know how to fight, and how to survive. But I also know my limitations. Unfortunately, the idea of limitations is often left out of self-defense training. It then succeeds only in providing a false sense of security to a child and his parents.

As well, many people assume that if you teach someone to physically defend himself, he not only can, but will. This is simply not true.

We've all heard of "fight or flight," the term used to describe how a surge of adrenaline in the body will make someone react when faced with a threat or other dangerous situation. Some people will fight through a situation, while others will forget everything they know and simply run for safety as quickly as they can.

If presented with a dangerous situation, will your child fight through it or run for safety? I hope it is the latter. Your child has one job when it comes to physically defending himself: to get away. The less physical contact he has with an attacker, the more likely he will escape safely. And he certainly doesn't need to "finish him off," as many television shows and movies present as not only possible but acceptable. I have seen movies profile a single powerful teenager who can defeat an army of men. What do kids think when they watch these kinds of heroes? Are they fantasizing about using their newfound self-defense skills? No doubt we have all dreamed at one time or another of being a hero. But that is not reality, and in fact it is dangerous ground for your child to tread.

I am not suggesting that there is no place for self-defense in child safety, but you should consider self-defense as the last resort. When everything else has failed, there are no rules for escape. Anything goes. (See blitz attacks in chapter four.)

Before self-defense becomes necessary, what will protect children is their ability to develop a keen sense of awareness, observation skills, and self-control. Most important, they must be taught to listen to their instincts. It is this element that needs to be taught to every child because it addresses the problem before it is too late, before the perpetrator is close enough to physically control his victim. Learning to read the signs and predict violence is not about how to react when an attacker is standing right next to your child, it is about how he got from across the room or park to standing next to your child in the first place. It is this window of time that is crucial. To wait until your child needs to physically defend himself is simply too late.

Let's face it. Everywhere you turn these days you are bombarded with evidence of another danger lying in wait for your kids. From predators lurking on the Internet, to bullies and hate-motivated violence, we are reminded daily that society has changed.

So must the tactics we use to protect kids. Remember these key points.

1. Promise your children that you will never send someone for them if you have not told them first, or told a person that they trust.
2. Teach your kids never to go anywhere with anyone without asking permission first.
3. Use unique symbols instead of your child's name to identify belongings.
4. Tell your children that when they need help, they should seek out only trusted adults.
5. Always keep the lines of communication open.

Focus on your surroundings and the people in them. Listen to your instincts, and teach your children to listen to theirs.

Chapter Three

The Predator's Bag of Tricks

A predator has just moved into my neighborhood. I don't know what to do or what to tell my kids. It frightens me to think that he's out there and may hurt another child, maybe mine.

Here's a test. Decide whether the following statement is true or false: There are more people who will help your children than hurt them.

The answer is true, absolutely. Yet what I am about to say is also true.

There are monsters among us. Some I have met, some I have investigated, and others I have studied. I have seen people commit the most horrific and violent crimes against one another, and witnessed intense suffering among the survivors. I would not wish what I have seen to be part of anyone's memory.

Aside from the crimes, I have also seen real-life heroes. I have witnessed people risking their lives to save someone they had never met. I have watched communities band together to keep their homes, neighborhoods, and children safe from potential threats, and I have seen children and teenagers do more to protect their friends and neighbors than any monster could ever destroy. I know in my heart there are more heroes than monsters in this world.

As a former police officer and child safety advocate, I am aware of the monsters; I have to be. As a concerned parent, you also must accept that there are people who are dangerous to your family. There is no way to know who the monsters are simply by the way they look. But their actions will send you the warning signals you need to protect yourself and your children. You have a natural ability to sense danger; you just have to ensure that you are open to receive it.

In his bestselling book *The Gift of Fear,* Gavin de Becker, who is one of the leading threat assessors in North America, explains that anyone can recognize violent, dangerous people and situations because "there is no mystery of human behavior that cannot be solved inside your head or your heart." In other words, each one of us is capable of feeling or imagining the whole range of human emotions, and we can and should use our imaginations to predict violence in others—and avoid it.

In learning to predict violent behavior, it's important not to focus solely on the fact that there may be dangerous people in your neighborhood. It's much more effective to turn your attention inward, to develop the skills that make you a safe parent. One of those skills is the ability to separate perceived danger from the real thing and have the courage to act when necessary.

Perceived Danger, Real Danger: Which Is It?

In May 2003, the country was stunned by the horrific abduction and murder of a beautiful and innocent eleven-year-old girl, Holly Jones, from a Toronto neighborhood.

Soon after, the Toronto Police Service announced that there were upward of 200 sex offenders living in the same neighborhood where Holly Jones was abducted. The community was paralyzed. Parents, neighbors, and educators gathered to review safety initiatives and to try to make sense of this horrible fact that had suddenly incited a storm of paranoia.

Questions were abundant. Who were these sex offenders and where did they live? How could the police allow them to live in the community? Will my children ever be safe again? How can we protect ourselves from so many predators?

Admittedly, the statistic is alarming, but what was more alarming was the way it was catapulted into an already suffering community. It came with no warning, had little explanation, and served no other purpose than to increase fear to an all-time high. Real estate values decreased, habits changed, and everyone became suspicious of neighbors.

What was not clearly explained by the media was that many types of sexual offenses are encompassed in the figure of 200 sexual offenders. Some offenses are far less serious than that of the monster who took the life of Holly Jones.

For example, it is a crime for a man to pinch a woman's bottom without her consent. That action can lead to a criminal charge of "sexual assault." Although it is still a crime, and often disturbing for the victim, it is reasonable to surmise that the bottom-pinching offender is vastly different from Michael Briere, the first-time offender later convicted of abducting and molesting Holly—and then murdering her as well. There were not over 200 murderous child sexual molesters living within the same neighborhood as Holly Jones. There were over 200 "sexual offenders." This is quite different, but was unfortunately not explained.

It is easy to become obsessed with facts and statistics that lead you to believe there is imminent danger. But quite often these statistics are served up to the public because they sell papers, or increase viewership. There will always be threats to your safety—this is true. You need to be able to push aside the ones that are unlikely to affect your family so that you can fully see the ones that are truly dangerous.

Dangerous people can be any sex, age, race, or size, and they may be present in a number of situations. It may be the drunk driver who causes a car accident, a terrorist who may take innocent lives to achieve his political agenda, or a seasoned criminal who may be released back into your community.

Canada has a unique criminal justice system that is designed to be representative of our society: fair, equal, and protecting the rights of both the accused and victims. In theory, at least. American-based television often leads people to believe that our two countries have similar laws and enforcement, but I can tell you that they are vastly different.

A criminal in Canada, regardless of what crimes he has committed, cannot be sentenced to 957 years in jail, which is the sentence handed down to Jeffrey Dahmer, the serial killer from Milwaukee. A life sentence in Canada is twenty-five years minimum; there is no chance of parole until twenty-five years have been served. A person can receive three life sentences, if they commit three crimes that warrant this term. But that does not mean the criminal would spend seventy-five years in prison before becoming eligible for parole. They would serve the three life sentences concurrently, meaning all at one time. The minimum total they would serve would still be twenty-five years.

Now, there are a couple of factors that can mitigate the length of time the criminal actually spends in jail. In the most straightforward scenario, a convicted criminal serves the entire twenty-five years in prison. He may or may not accept counseling or other forms of professional treatment, and eventually he is simply released into the general population.

A criminal who has served his entire sentence can be released without further conditions. This means no parole and no monitoring. However, if convicted of a life sentence, he will remain on parole for the rest of his life unless it is revoked.

Many inmates who are not serving life sentences are released on parole and placed in transition houses, which are located strategically in communities across the country. Upon their release, these individuals must continue to abide by the rules set out by the court for a designated length of time. This system is intended to ease inmates back into society, and to offer the criminal justice system some authority to monitor the actions and behavior of newly released inmates. If they reoffend, or breach a condition of their release, they are returned to prison.

But some simply never get out. A person can be so dangerous that the police can make an application to the courts for "dangerous offender status." The tricky part is that the application has to be made based on the facts of the last crime the offender committed. This crime would need to be a serious violent crime, such as murder, or any other violent crime that results in a ten-year sentence. If the crime does not meet this requirement, there is no authority to apply for dangerous offender status.

If a criminal is labeled a dangerous offender, he will remain in prison for an indefinite period of time, or until the National Parole Board decides that he no longer poses a risk to the community to reoffend. Most dangerous offenders do not have the chance to see a parole board until they have already served an average of seventeen years. Many of them simply never get out of jail.

So what qualifies someone to be a dangerous offender? There are several different criteria that have to be met. Usually, the offender must have committed a very serious offense, demonstrate a pattern of showing no restraint, and show no remorse for his crimes. The judge can then decide that the offender is too dangerous to be released and will keep him in jail indefinitely.

A good example of an offender who "achieved" dangerous offender status is the serial child killer Clifford Olson. In the years that he was at large and murdering his victims, he changed the way many families lived and played in British Columbia. Convicted and imprisoned in 1982, he has plenty of company in the dangerous offender "club," including the notorious Paul Bernardo.

I remember what it was like to be a teenager in B.C. in 1981, when Olson was prowling that westernmost province of Canada. I remember seeing the pages in the newspaper, warning us of this monster among us. In fact, a young boy who lived in the next town was lured away and murdered by Olson. We were told to stay in groups, not to accept rides from strangers, and of course not to talk to strangers.

Over the course of one terrifying and horrific year, Clifford Olson took the lives of eleven children. He was convicted of all eleven murders and sentenced to a minimum of twenty-five years in prison. After seventeen years in jail, he applied for early parole under the "faint hope" clause of the Canadian Criminal Code. Any criminal serving a life sentence can take advantage of this clause, which simply means that he may apply for an early parole hearing if he can make a valid claim to no longer pose a risk to society. The criminal appears before a panel of civilians, not judicial officials, and even in the rare instances that the panel decides to allow the inmate to move forward in the process, he must still appear before the National Parole Board, which may or may not grant him early parole.

Fortunately, and also unsurprisingly, Olson was denied. He can reapply for parole again in 2006. However, Olson has been declared a dangerous offender, which means that he will remain in prison unless and until the National Parole Board decides it is safe to release him into the community. If our Parole Board continues to do its job well, this will never happen. As of 1999, the latest year for which statistics were available, some 247 people were classified as dangerous offenders in Canada, with almost half coming from the province of Ontario. It is estimated that in 2001 there were approximately 280 dangerous offenders, according to the solicitor general of Canada.

Although simply knowing about these dangerous offenders can be scary, they do not pose a risk to you or your family, since they are behind bars and will almost certainly stay there. This is a good example of perceived rather than real danger.

There are cases, however, in which someone continues to commit violent crimes over and over again, but nothing long term is done to protect the public from this individual. Take a recent case, for example.

On July 7, 2004, a predator and potentially dangerous criminal was released into a southwestern Ontario community. This man had spent almost half his life in prison by committing a variety of offenses that resulted in a startling sixty-three convictions.

He had told prison doctors that he wanted to be known as the most prolific serial killer in Canadian, if not North American, history. He told numerous doctors, family members, inmates, and guards that he intended to kill, rape, and wreak havoc on the community when he got out.

He was being released because he had completed his sentence and the criminal justice system no longer had any authority over him. Police had not applied for dangerous offender status because, based on the last offense he was convicted of and the sentence he received, the criminal did not qualify. He was free to live in the community. Luckily, his time out of prison was short-lived. Within twelve hours of his release, he was arrested for uttering threats to a news reporter. He was returned to jail, at least for a couple more years, at which time he will again be released.

This man was just one among the hundreds of serious offenders who are released throughout Canada every year. In some cases, police may believe that an individual poses a very high risk to reoffend, but they must release him because his jail time has been served.

In order to protect communities, police have the right to post media notices that will warn people about the dangers posed by a newly released individual. This is called high-risk-offender notification. All police departments in Canada have this authority under the Freedom of Information and Privacy Act, though not all departments use it. There is a fine line between the individual's right to privacy and the protection of society. To those who believe that the criminal's rights outweigh your child's right to safety, I suggest that they offer their homes to the criminals to stay.

I have absolutely no sympathy for predators, and I believe in public warnings for high-risk sex-offender releases. At this time, the only governments that actively maintain a notification system are Alberta's (http://www.justice.gov.ab.ca) and Manitoba's (www.gov.mb.ca). If you live in either of these provinces, you'll find these websites to be ideal resources to learn about the real dangers that may be in your communities.

Most high-risk offenders end up back in prison shortly after their release. This is both good and bad. Good, for the obvious reason that they no longer pose a risk to your family's safety. Bad, because a victim was likely made in the process.

If your local police department chooses to release information about a high-risk offender, pay attention. Use the opportunity to review personal safety with your family. High-risk offenders released into your community should be considered a real danger, and extra precautions should be taken when dealing with them.

But what about the criminal who poses a risk to your children, but has not been labeled a high-risk offender? How can you find out if such criminals are in your community? Unfortunately, unless you have personal knowledge, you can't. I received the following e-mail from a mom who was very worried about a predator in her small community.

We are now facing something in our neighborhood that is very unsettling. There is a pedophile living here. I know this because my friend's thirteen-year-old daughter is a victim. They are currently in the court process, which seems to take forever. He apparently has an affinity for blondes, so as a deterrent she has dyed her hair brown. She is his second victim that we know about.

He started stalking her when she was eleven. She was wise enough to know that he was stalking her and went to her parents. They didn't believe her at first, but after it escalated to the point that he followed her everywhere, they took notice. He followed her to school, to the park, to the store . . . anywhere he could find her. Thankfully, she was aware of her surroundings at all times, never took short cuts, stuck to main roads, and would then cut through the park that backs onto her yard so that he wouldn't know exactly which house she lived in. All of his past charges ranged from sexual interference to sexual assault, but all were reduced to simple assault.

I know that neighbors of his eventually moved to avoid the problems he was causing for their two little girls. Both parents went to him and threatened him. He didn't listen. Sadly, I do not believe they reported this behavior to the police.

As alarming as it may sound, this woman is one of the lucky ones. She knows who the bad guy is. If you have been given information about a dangerous person in your community, you and your family can prepare for the threat. It is the ones that you have not been made aware of that are a greater cause for concern.

Predators, as in this case, are not just abductors. A predator is anyone who preys on others in a calculated, routine fashion. The predator may include the abuser, pedophile, bully, stalker, or thief.

But before the predator—or any criminal—can commit a crime, a number of elements must be in place.

1. Intent. The offender must have the desire or intention to commit the crime. The motives may vary, but the intention must be present in order for the crime to happen.

2. Ability. The offender must believe that he has the skills and equipment he needs to carry out the crime. In the case of physical assault of any kind, he not only needs to believe he has the skills to commit the crime, but that his outweighs the defensive skill of the chosen victim. Children are easy targets for adults.

3. Opportunity. The criminal needs an opportunity to commit the crime and get away with it. Few criminals commit crimes with the intention of getting caught.

You, as a parent, can't change a potential offender's intention to commit a crime, nor can you change the offender's perception of his or her abilities. However, you have complete control over the opportunities that could make your child the next victim.

Opportunity Equals Access

How will a predator gain access to my child?

An offender needs to have access to your child before he can commit his intended crime. He may gain access through his position as a coach, babysitter, relative, neighbor, friend, or acquaintance. What he is not likely to be is a total stranger. As a parent, you have complete control over your child's safety and can prevent a crime from happening if you are watchful and diligent in controlling the access that others have to your kids. These are the basic ways in which you can make sure that any access to your children is safe access.

1. Evaluate those in your home or neighborhood. You must assess each and every person you allow into your home or in contact with your children. I am not suggesting a full criminal screening for the gardener; however, I do suggest that you watch how he interacts with your children. If he shows too much attention to them, if your child is uncomfortable around him, if you have even the slightest reservation about him, get rid of him immediately.

2. Question everyone's motives. There is a motive for every action or thought we have. Not all motives are deviant, but they are present in all actions. A used car salesman's motive is to sell you a car. To achieve that purpose, he will adapt his behavior to be approachable, knowledgable, and genial, in hopes that you will buy a car from him.

A teacher's motive is to educate your children. Her behavior will reflect her motives. She may be firm when she is trying to get a point across, sympathetic to a child who is upset, encouraging and empowering to get kids to learn.

A predator's motive is to gain access to and control of your child so that he can carry out his intended crime. His behavior will reflect his motives—in part. He will be helpful, understanding, generous, accommodating, and anything else to convince you that he can be trusted.

If you can't come up with a valid reason why someone is acting in a friendly, generous way to your children, be very suspicious. There is no reason why the house painter needs to be giving toys and candy to your children. There is a motive for every action. If the person's actions do not make sense, do not allow him access to your children.

3. Report your suspicions to the police. I spoke at length with the writer of the story above and learned that the predator had a track record of inappropriate, and likely criminal, behavior. Other parents who lived in the tiny community knew of him as well and often shared their concerns about his behavior toward children. But they never shared their concerns with the police. The writer described numerous incidents in which parents did not report their concerns to the police.

How many times have you seen or heard news reports in which neighbors of an apprehended criminal say they thought the person was suspicious? If they thought so, why didn't they tell police before another victim was made? Contrary to what you may think, your observations are valuable to the police, and they are not bothered if you call them. In fact, in an age when money is tight and police are stretched to the limit, they need your help. They cannot know what is going on in your community unless you tell them. You don't even have to give your name. If police investigate and the suspicion is unfounded, then it ends. However, in many cases—and I can speak from experience—the smallest tip can lead to a major arrest and removal of a predator from your community.

It is your right and your duty to tell the police if you feel someone may be dangerous to your family. You owe it, at the very least, to your kids.

4. Tell others about your suspicions. Your neighbors, friends, relatives, and anyone else you think may come in contact with this person need to be told about your concerns. Be careful not to cross the line and actually defame the person. Your intent is not to cause him to lose his job, spouse or destroy his livelihood, but to express your concerns over his behavior. Your suspicions are not proof, simply suspicions. But if you believe strongly that someone is dangerous, so much so that you keep your kids away from that person, then you should be telling others how you feel. Information sharing is the key to protecting your family and others. You can prevent someone else from becoming a predator's next victim if you just express yourself.

A Predator's Tricks

A predator's motive is to gain access and control over your child. In order to succeed, he must first gain her trust. He will use a set of tricks that are designed to disguise his motives and convince the child that he can be trusted. Rarely is violence used to take a child. It isn't needed: kids are easily tricked, and quite often go willingly with their attackers.

Predators spend their time learning what kids like, what interests them, and ways to lure them away. There are organizations around the world that regularly promote new and effective ways to approach children. Some such organizations are NAMBLA (North American Man/Boy Love Association) and PAN (Pedophile Alert Network, based in the Netherlands). The ostensible purpose of these organizations is to work toward decriminalizing sexual relationships between adult males and boys. They believe that children can enter into mutually consensual sexual relationships with adults, and that becoming sexual with a boy is loving, not abusive. They consider themselves legitimate gay organizations, but as organizations that promote pedophilia, they are offensive to many homosexual males. They share tips with one another about how to lure young boys into sexual relationships. They hold conventions, and have brochures, regular newsletters, and lists of suggested reading materials.

They are able to exist because most countries recognize, in their constitutions, the right to freedom of speech and to hold opinions. However, many of their actions can be criminal. Members of

NAMBLA have been arrested and imprisoned for sexual assault and possession of child pornography, among other crimes. NAMBLA has been featured on *America's Most Wanted* and has been a target of many police operations over the years.

The following list shows the most frequently used methods for luring children into trusting relationships with predators. Often, they are used in combination.

1. Asking for help. Kids love to please, especially to please adults. The younger they are, the more they want to help and be praised for their efforts. This trick is used in two ways: it allows the predator to approach the child physically, and opens an opportunity for conversation.

A predator may ask a child for directions, most often to a place they know a child will be familiar with, such as McDonald's or a toy store. He knows not to ask for the hardware store, because a child will not be able to help and the conversation will be terminated. He may also ask for help in looking for his lost child or lost pet, carrying heavy bags into his home, holding a car door open, or anything else he believes will give him the opportunity to gain access to the child.

A predator may not ask for help; instead, he may offer it. He is always looking for an opportunity to gain access and commit his crime. Some predators look for children who are momentarily vulnerable, such as a child who has fallen, appears lost, or needs assistance.

Children must be taught that an adult should never ask them for help. If they are approached by someone they do not know and trust, they must not go with them without asking your permission first. This rule is never to be broken. If the child believes the person, and wants to help look for the lost pet, for instance, your child should come to you, the parent, and ask permission. It is then within your control. If the need for help is legitimate, the person will wait. If it is not, he will be gone. It is now time to report the incident to the police immediately.

2. Creating panic. Even adults panic in emergency situations, so it's easy to see how effective this trick can be with children.

Predators know that children are taught to listen and follow direction in an emergency. Children are led through fire and safety drills several times a year.

What happens if there is an emergency that involves someone they love? Like you. How would your child feel if someone were to run up to him, in a panic, and tell him that you had been in a car accident and were in the hospital? The person explains that he is there to pick up the child and take him to the hospital to see you.

Would your child panic and forget your promise that you would never send anyone for him without telling him first? Would he be so worried about you that he would go with this person?

The trick of an emergency situation is effective for many reasons. It catches your child off guard, sets off a panic that is meant to make him forget his safety rules, and tugs on his heartstrings. It is an effective trick, but not perfect.

Talk to your children about any emergency situation and what you would expect them to do. Reinforce your promise to them and remind them of the rule to never go anywhere with anyone without asking first. There is no need for a code word. Just trust between you and them.

3. Abusing a position of authority or posing as an authority. Several years ago, a young girl was in a convenience store in a small but transient neighborhood. She had been in this store many times in the past, but on this visit she decided to shoplift a tube of lip gloss.

She found the exact flavor she wanted, and after making sure no one was looking, she stuffed it into the pocket of her jeans and walked out the door. Moments later, a man grabbed her by the arm. He told her that he was store security and that she was under arrest for shoplifting. She was terrified. She knew that her parents would punish her and she hated being in trouble. The man sensed her fear and decided to play on it. He told her that he was going to call the police, as well as her parents and her school. She would probably be kicked out of school, maybe even go to jail. She was in serious trouble, or so the security guard led her to believe.

She pleaded with him not to tell her parents or call the police, and of course she offered to return the unused lip gloss. After a few minutes of crying and pleading with the security guard, she seemed to be gaining his sympathy. He told her that he would give her a break, but just this one time. He went on to tell her that he could lose his job for letting her go, but that she seemed like a nice kid and deserved a break. However, he had to fudge the paperwork somehow and he needed to think about a way to do that. He told her that he was off work at 8 p.m., and she needed to come back then to settle the paperwork. She was told not to tell anyone though, because if his boss found out he would be fired, and his boss would surely call the police to report her theft. She agreed. He let her go.

She returned later that night hoping to sign the papers and quickly return home, her parents none the wiser.

He was waiting for her outside in his pickup truck. He waved her over and told her to get in. She did. He drove her to an abandoned building, sexually assaulted her, and left her beaten and terrified.

He wasn't a security guard at all. He was a predator, waiting for an opportunity. She gave it to him.

This is a tragic story that illustrates the trick of authority. Children are told from a very young age to listen to adults, do what they are told, especially with people in positions of authority. Your child may have a more encompassing view of authority figures than you, an adult. A child may see not only police officers but also teachers, doctors, coaches, and any other adult as authority figures.

How would your children react if someone they recognized as an authority told them to do something? Would they have the confidence to say no if it felt wrong? Give them permission to say no to people in authority if necessary. This does not mean they should be defiant or disobedient to their teachers at school, but if they are told to do something that feels wrong to them, they need to know that you will support their decision.

Many children, like the young girl in the story above, choose not to go to their parents for help, because she feared discipline or rejection. You can overcome this by reminding your children that they can come to you no matter what, even when they may be afraid of disappointing you. It is vital that your kids know that you will still love them unconditionally, and that you put their safety and well-being ahead of anything else.

4. Threats. Threats of violence are not often used at first contact. Children, like most people, respond better to a friendly approach. If a predator needs to use violence from the onset, he is likely acting impetuously and perhaps less skilled at persuading others to trust him. He will likely resort to a blitz attack and hope for the best.

Being threatened with violence is frightening to anyone, even more so to children. But you can control your fear if you remember that a threat is just the verbalization of a frightening thought—it has not happened and may never happen. A threat is uttered with the intention of making the child do what the predator wants. Often the predator does not have a clear escape plan, or needs the cooperation of the child to effect his crime. So he threatens.

Children need to understand that a threat is not a real thing happening at that moment. In the case of a predator, a threat is a trick to make children respond quickly and cooperatively.

Because it is a trick, children should be taught that a predator's threat should never be considered. Explain to children that if a predator threatens to use a weapon to coerce them, the weapon is meant to intimidate them. Tell your child not to believe the offender's threats that he will use the weapon. Above all, your child must know that he should not get into the predator's car, or go with him anywhere.

Instead, children need to do whatever it takes to get away. There are no rules to escaping. They should make as much noise as they can (even though the predator has warned them not to) and fight for their lives.

Threats of violence are not the only types of threats that can be used to control or manipulate a child. Predators who have developed an abusive relationship with a child victim over a period of time may threaten the child with exposure. A predator may threaten to tell the child's friends, parents, or other family members what they have been doing. Often, in the course of an abusive relationship, a predator will have introduced cigarettes, drugs, or alcohol, not only to reduce the inhibitions of the child, but to use as a future threat. He will remind the child of their illegal activities and threaten to call the police. Of course, the predator would never fulfill his threat, for obvious reasons, but the child does not know that. Fear of exposure can make it almost impossible for a child to speak out about the abuse she is suffering.

Predators will at times make threats against their victim's families, friends, or pets. This is effective for two reasons: the child will do anything to prevent his loved ones from being harmed, and by keeping silent the child feels that he is protecting others. This is often found in cases of family sexual abuse; for instance, when one daughter allows the offender to abuse her because she hopes that doing so will prevent her younger sister from being abused as well.

Talk to your kids. Make sure they understand that you will accept them for whatever they do, whether it is good or bad. Children need to know that your love is unconditional and that you will listen to them and help them before judging or punishing them.

5. Gifts, Money, and Bribes. The number-one trick to lure a child away is money. Children are not much different from adults when it comes to the need and want for money. Just turn on your TV and see how many people are running around the world, or agreeing to be stranded on an island, or putting up with humiliations that no self-respecting person would endure. All for money.

Many predators will target the children of single parents, or families from lower-income communities. In lower-income housing projects, it is common to find many children who have little to no parental supervision. Their parents are either working or absent. The children are needy, both financially and emotionally. These areas are perfect fishing grounds for the predator, who can lavish children with what they need and want—and all he'll ask in return are a few "favors."

How much easier could it be, really? The predator is kind, and the adults he comes into contact with think of him as a grandfatherly type. He showers the children with attention, money, toys, and candy. The kids just love him.

If you see or hear of a situation like this, you should also be hearing alarm bells. There is no reason why someone should be giving money to your children unless he is buying a chocolate bar for a school fundraiser. There is no reason he should be giving presents to children unless it is a birthday and the parents have agreed to accept them. There is no reason he should enjoy the company of children more than adults . . . that is, unless he is a predator . . .

Children should not accept gifts from anyone unless their parents agree, and it is an appropriate time to be receiving a gift, such as birthdays, holidays, and special occasions. "Just because I like you" is not appropriate.

With each gift a child accepts, the family and child become more indebted to the predator. Eventually, the predator will expect a payback—usually paid back by the child, through pornography, abuse, and molestation.

Although money, gifts, and candy are very appealing, children must understand that there can be dangerous motives behind some gifts. If someone offers to give them something for no good reason, children should tell their parents immediately. As a parent, if your child suddenly has money, a new toy, or any other goodie that you did not buy, find out immediately where it came from.

6. Promises of Fame and Fortune. Almost anyone would find it hard to resist an offer of fame and fortune. The idea of enormous wealth, recognition, and adoration is the formula for most childhood dreams. We all want to be loved and valued, and for parents, the thought of having a famous child conjures up an entirely new set of fantasies.

Unfortunately, predators know the appeal that fame carries with it, and they also know that some people will do just about anything to get it.

But not all predators kill their victims. Many lure them away, assault them, and release them. The entertainment industry is notorious for predators who slither in and convince naive wannabes that they can be stars. They prey on people's dreams and create their own opportunities to commit their crimes.

Modeling, acting, sports—all have their share of these parasites. With only a business card and a convincing story, many kids and their parents are hooked. Parents are often so unfamiliar with the industry that they don't know how to confirm if someone is legitimate.

If your child is ever approached by a talent scout, agent, photographer, or other so-called industry professional, do not allow her to meet with them alone. Always ask for references, and always call them. If the person is adamant that your child come alone, take it as a clear red flag, and do not permit your child to go. You should instead call the police.

Predators have a bag of tricks they use to convince children they can be trusted. It is not often that violence is needed to lure a child away; instead, well-crafted manipulation easily convinces an unprepared child to willingly leave with a predator. In fighting the predator's manipulations, my advice is always the same: Trust your instinct: it is always right. Violence is preventable; knowledge is the key.

Chapter Four

Abduction:
Every Parent's Nightmare

I am a mother of two girls, ages six and nine. Ever since the news of that girl being abducted from her bed in Toronto, I can't sleep. I wake up every night at least a couple of times because I am so afraid that someone is going to break in and abduct my girls. I live on the ground floor, but all of my windows lock properly. My kids are also scared. I am so tired and frightened all the time.

I can't think of two words that conjure up fear and anxiety as effortlessly as the words *child abduction*. Child abduction is so terrifying that it is easy to let your imagination propel you into a heightened sense of panic and fear. When news of a child abduction surfaces, every parent shudders. Questions arise, and suddenly child safety is talked about in the headlines and over water coolers across the country and beyond. Every parent wonders the same thing: could that have been my child?

It's my guess that it would take you only a few minutes to think of at least one child lost to abduction. Many come to my mind, not because they are so common but rather because they are so rare. If you were to see all the names and ages of the eleven children abducted and murdered in Canada in the last twenty-six years, it would no doubt weigh as heavily on your heart as it does on mine. However, when you think of the dangers to your own children, it is vital that you continue to distinguish between real and perceived risk.

One child victim of abduction is too many—*because the crime can be predicted and prevented.* To prevent it, you must be open to the warning signs, you must listen to your instincts, and you must refuse to live in fear.

If you fear everything, you will never be able to distinguish the real dangers from the perceived ones. Every small oddity will cause you to panic and take action, perhaps the wrong action. Instead, you need to build your knowledge base now, and not wait until another child has been abducted. You can start building this knowledge— and reducing your fears—by learning the facts behind the myths.

Stranger Abductions

It is alarming how many parents—more than two-thirds of all parents, according to some studies—worry about their children being abducted by strangers.

The truth is that your child is at far greater risk of personal injury due to traffic accidents than of being abducted by a stranger, yet you probably put him into a car every day. The difference is the feeling of control, or lack of it. But when it comes to the danger of abduction, you have more control than you think. Here is what's behind the statistics and mixed messages on abduction.

In Canada, criminal statistics are first reported through the police as crimes occur and are investigated. The police then enter details about each crime into a national database called the Canadian Police Information Centre (CPIC). Every police agency must contribute to CPIC.

The statistics for child abduction come from this reporting system. They are collected by a national organization run by the RCMP called the National Missing Children's Registry. This is roughly equivalent to the National Center for Missing and Exploited Children (NCMEC) in the United States. Established as a private, non-profit organization in 1984, NCMEC provides services nation-wide to families and professionals in the prevention of crimes against children, including abduction and sexual exploitation. (You can visit their website at www.missingkids.org for some fantastic articles and free publications that discuss many different child safety issues.)

Each year, the RCMP Missing Children's Registry completes an annual report of statistical findings. These findings cover all topics relating to missing kids, including runaways, kids who wander off, and, of course, abductions. You can view these reports online at www.ourmissingchildren.gc.ca/omc/publications/index_e.htm. The following table is a ten-year summary.

Canadian Case Summary of 2003 Missing Children Reports
CPIC Transaction Reports for a Ten-Year Period

Year	Kidnap	PA	Run	Unknown	Acc	Wander	Other	Total
2003	39	358	53459	10922	21	805	2205	67809
2002	35	429	52390	10994	38	594	2052	66532
2001	48	387	53434	10364	49	742	1990	66994
2000	42	416	50633	10031	35	597	1958	63712
1999	52	358	47585	9884	38	496	1947	60360
1998	42	426	48388	10254	28	623	2326	62087
1997	60	426	45527	9404	37	506	2138	58098
1996	45	409	43717	9181	34	822	1914	56122
1995	68	354	43709	9039	35	720	1824	55749
1994	68	394	40140	8901	24	672	1774	51973
1993	61	407	43102	9959	26	543	1810	55908

1. **Kidnap,** kidnapping/stranger abduction; **PA,** parental abduction; **Run,** runaways; **Acc,** accident; **Wander,** wandered off.

Source: CPIC annual transaction report for 2003, M.L. Dalley

The table tells us that in 2003 there were thirty-nine reported child kidnappings and stranger abductions in Canada. This number had increased by four from thirty-five the year before.

Abduction: Every Parent's Nightmare

Every year, when the total number of stranger abductions in Canada is released from this public document, questions and fears are stirred up across the country. How is it that so many children are being abducted, but so few have been widely reported? You would think all child abductions by a stranger would warrant national media attention.

And thirty-nine kids abducted by strangers in only one year? I can see why you might be worried—that's a lot of kids. Looking at a few other tables on the website, we can see that out of the thirty-nine abductions, twenty-four of the children were female and fifteen were male. We can also see that Ontario accounted for the most abductions at thirteen; British Columbia trailed slightly at eleven; and Quebec had an alarming ten children abducted by strangers. Yet you can probably think of only one or two names or stories behind these numbers. Here's why.

A "stranger," as defined by these widely used and misused statistics, is *anyone* other than a parent or guardian to the child. That means that the abductor, whom you might reasonably expect to be a complete stranger, may in fact be a neighbor, friend, relative, boyfriend, babysitter—anyone who is not a parent.

This is significant to understand when putting the fear of stranger abduction into perspective. Kids are not being abducted by complete strangers in such large numbers. They are being abducted, hurt, and often murdered by people they know. To make this clear, I don't call these tragedies "stranger abductions." Instead, I call them "non-parental abductions."

Understanding the definition of what a stranger is in these studies is crucial. Although it does not diminish the tragedy of each incident—after all, a child was still taken—it allows you, the parent, to clearly view what is a real danger to your kids. Strangers are likely not the true evil your kids face. You should focus on those people you choose to allow into your family and your children's lives.

Not yet convinced how rare stranger abductions really are? Try this.

In the most recent study conducted by the National Missing Children's Registry, missing children cases from across Canada were studied from the years 2000 and 2001. In these years there were a total of ninety police reports across Canada that had been classified as a "stranger abduction." On closer examination, however, only five cases were identified as *true* stranger abductions or high-profile abductions. The other eighty-five were either entered into the system incorrectly, or the victim and the abductor knew each other. Yet those eighty-five cases were included in the frightening statistics you read in the papers.

A "true stranger abduction" is a confirmed abduction by a stranger as you and I would define one. That is, someone you do not know, and have never met. A "high-profile case" is a case that has received national media attention.

What were the details of those five cases? In keeping with overall kidnapping trends, all of the children were girls, and they ranged in age from five to ten years old. Two of the children were abducted from inside the family home, and one from the family's yard. The fourth child was taken while playing in a parking lot close to home, and the last was taken on the way to school. Four of the five children were sexually assaulted and later killed, and one was released unharmed. Four of the abductors were male, and one female. The female abductor was the only one who released her victim unharmed. In four of the five cases, the abductor was either a friend of the mother or father, a neighbor, or babysitter, and almost all the offenders had prior criminal records.

It is hard to hear about cases such as these. It is painful to consider such inhumanity. But it is too easy to focus on the horror, too easy to shut down, lock up, and live in fear. What you need to do instead is focus on the true dangers that face your children, and you can reduce the risks. You actually have more control over the risk of abduction than you think.

Who Is Preying on Our Fears?

We live in a society that loves to count and measure. But I always question the value of statistics, mainly because the integrity of any statistic depends on the motivation of the reporting agency. Why count something if you don't care what the result is? A statistic is developed for many reasons, many of which are for the gain of the group completing the study.

I am not suggesting that child abduction statistics are manipulated, but I am saying that you need to find out what's behind the statistics, and evaluate the risk from an informed point of view. Unfortunately, at the moment, statistics about so-called stranger abductions are too often tossed around without much explanation.

All forms of media share equally in the blame for this. In the media's attempt to capture an audience, many rely on fear and shock to sell a story. Don't get me wrong, though: It is not that individual members of the media want to mislead the public. I have had the pleasure and honor of meeting some of the best journalists in the business, and I have seen their integrity. However, journalists don't have complete control over the direction of a story; editors, publishers, and producers have a say as well. And these people have stories to sell, people to answer to, financial projections to meet. A great story is one of tragedy, filled with emotions like anger and fear. Child abduction tops the list of great stories.

I understand the need to report incidents like child abduction. I am a firm believer in sharing information and the need for community support and involvement to keep kids safe. But the information needs to be complete. Alarming but incomplete statistics are misleading and frightening, and they do nothing but feed paranoia. Knowledge is empowering, but only if it is accurate and explained.

The media are not the only ones cashing in on our fears of stranger abduction.

Not long ago, I was appalled to read that a major insurance agency was proud to be offering a new type of homeowners' insurance for crimes that included "child abduction." This policy would cover expenses such as improving security around your home, reward money, any psychological treatment that you and your family might need if your child were abducted, to name a few. It is promoted as providing "further peace of mind for our clients in an increasingly turbulent world." In their advertisement, the insurance agency used the same alarmingly high statistics that we looked at earlier, in this case for the sole purpose of creating a false sense of need in consumers.

I apologize to any insurance agents who feel that parents should pay into such a plan, but I strongly disagree. You do not need child abduction insurance. It will not keep your kids safe, nor should it give you peace of mind. Spend your money elsewhere. Take your child out for a quiet lunch, just the two of you, and communicate. Talk with your child about what she likes, who her friends are, what her dreams are. Learn about what makes your child happy, what attracts her, what she fears. Predators know the value of understanding your children, and they will take all the time in the world to get to know them. To stay prepared, take the time to know your kids. This is a far better investment and will make a difference in your children's safety.

Finally, fear is exacerbated when you feel a total loss of control. Knowledge will give you the control you need. Here's what to know, and what to look for.

Abduction, Abductors, and Warning Signs
Non-parental abduction

By now, I hope I've convinced you that the chances of your child being abducted by a complete stranger are extraordinarily rare. Your child is at greater risk of abduction by someone you know, or who knows of you and your child. Even in the five cases I discussed earlier, all but one of the abductors were acquaintances of friends of the family, and not transient drifters as one might have thought.

It is difficult and frightening to realize that you could let someone dangerous into your child's life. After all, their safety is your primary concern. But here's the good news.

Violent crimes, including child abduction, are predictable 100 percent of the time. We already know that a predator will almost certainly have had prior contact with you or your family before choosing to abduct. If he has had contact, he will have displayed warning signs. If there are warning signs, you can predict that something may happen, and you can prepare to stop it.

There are warning signs in your environment, from the offender, and even from your child that when taken on their own can seem minor or unimportant. When taken together, however, they clearly signal that a dangerous person is in your family, or that your child is at risk of non-parental abduction.

Warning Signs: Offender-based
Profiles

We would all like to think that the only person who could possibly abduct a child would be an insane psychopath who despises children and gets pleasure from hurting them and their families.

If this were the case, it would seem easier to understand. Some child abductors are indeed psychopaths with no remorse or conscience, but many are not. According to the FBI, there are four different categories of child abductors.

1. Pedophiles, typically male, seek children for sexual gratification. They identify with children and focus on luring them away with tricks, gifts, bribes, or a combination of enticements. They feel a sense of attachment to children and may truly believe that they have children's best interests at heart. Pedophiles account for the largest number of non-family child abductors. (I discuss pedophiles in greater depth in chapter five.)

2. Profiteers abduct children for profit. They may trade them in underground child pornography rings, or sell them for adoption.

3. Serial killers focus on control and power, and are motivated by a fantasy. They plan well and are methodical.

4. Disturbed childless persons tend to abduct children because they have not been able to have their own or have recently lost a child. They are predominantly women.

Child abductors are seldom the creepy-dirty-old-man type that many people believe them to be. The average age of an abductor is only twenty-seven. Most are unmarried, unemployed, live with their parents, move residences often, and have histories of drug, alcohol, or sexual problems. They almost always have a violent past. These are all characteristics that, on their own, might mean little, but in combination should be considered warning signs.

Although women will abduct children, non-family abductions are typically committed by men.

Motivation and behavior

An offender will decide to abduct a child for reasons that correlate to the type of abductor he or she is. For example, a pedophile will abduct for sexual gratification; the profiteer will abduct for money or ransom; the childless person will abduct for emotional reasons; and a serial killer will abduct for power and the desire to kill. But there may be other reasons an offender decides to abduct a child, as when an abductor is seeking revenge on the parent.

Non-parental abductions are frequently based on sexual motivation, and therefore the abductor tends to try to develop ongoing communication and trust with his target. He will take "baby steps" and slowly test the child's willingness and vulnerability until he feels that he has the access he needs to escape with the child. Most non-parental abductions are the result of the predator luring the child away. Violence is often not needed.

Children are easily tricked into believing and trusting the abductor. This is usually because children are confused by the old lessons of not talking to strangers rather than knowing not to go anywhere with anyone without permission. Considering that the child has already likely met the predator at some time, persuading her to go along is quite an easy task.

A predator will often display inappropriate and ongoing attention to your children. He may relate better to your kids, take many photos, give them gifts, and work very hard at gaining their trust and acceptance, as well as yours. He will be vague about his past. He may display signs of having a controlling nature.

Warning Signs: Child-based

Before an offender decides to abduct a child, he needs to select a potential target and fantasize about the crime itself. He does this methodically, and sometimes years pass before he will gather the courage to attempt an abduction. Every type of abductor will first seek a target that fits his needs or holds some significance to him.

Child abductors do not typically, out of the blue, grab a child. There is little randomness to abduction, but often opportunity plays a significant role. Usually the crime has been planned and played out in the offender's fantasies many times, as he waits for an opportunity. A child, a location, opportunity, and a method are selected long before the offense occurs.

Children are targeted based on the type of abductor and the motivation. This is why it is important to always consider type and motivation while assessing your child's vulnerabilities. If an abductor has access to a child who meets his motivation, and that child has little supervision, he may attempt to abduct.

For an offender to successfully abduct your child, he has to have

- access to your child, usually with ongoing contact, so that he can begin to develop trust with your child
- opportunity, including lack of supervision
- the ability to commit the crime, including privacy and a means of escaping undetected

Predators choose their targets for a variety of reasons, but most begin with gender and age. Girls tend to be targeted three times more than boys, and school-aged children are the predominant age preference. They also look for children who are easy to persuade and ultimately control.

It is important to understand that the predator already comes with a set of criteria for his target that you can't change. If you have a twelve-year-old son, for instance, and a predator prefers to target twelve-year-old boys, there is nothing you can do to change the fact that your son matches his criteria. However, you do have control over when and where your child encounters others, the types of environments you allow him to enter, and even some measure of control over the personality traits that will make your child more or less vulnerable.

Location

A predator is much more likely to abduct a child from an area that he is familiar and comfortable with. He will choose an area where he feels safe from detection, and believes he will succeed. According to FBI studies, 80 percent of abductions take place within 450 meters of the last place the child was seen. This is usually their home, or somewhere in their neighborhood.

Kids are at greater risk of abduction if they

- are riding a bicycle alone, walking alone, or standing alone
- have their names printed on their belongings that are visible to a bystander
- are walking alone before or after normal school hours
- take short cuts that are isolated and remote

Time of day

Some studies suggest that the risk of any crime increases after dark and as a result, most people pay more attention to personal safety during the hours of darkness. However, children can be abducted any time of day or night. Parents need to be vigilant in ensuring that their children are well supervised at all times.

Environment

The number-one trick that predators will use to gain the trust of their targets, whether they are attempting to groom them for long-term abuse, or lure them away, is money. Children in lower-income or welfare-reliant families often need many things. They go without candy, toys, and the extras that they see other children with. Lower-income housing projects also typically have a large number of children who play unsupervised. Many of the people living there are highly transient, and a predator who moves often can easily go undetected. They will choose to live close by or within these same projects, where targets are in abundance.

Warning signs of a dangerous family environment include

- living in a transient neighborhood
- children are often unsupervised
- family frequently allows little-known people into the home, for example, tradespeople, travelers, short-term boarders

Child target profile

Predators not only look at environment, opportunity, motivation, and location, they are seeking a child who is easy to persuade, fearful, needy, and ultimately a terrible witness.

Although any child can be a target, and some studies suggest that predators do not take great care in selecting their victims, one certainty is that predators do not want to get caught. Successful child abductors select their targets well. There are specific characteristics that may put your child at risk.

1. Strong desire for physical affection and attention. Children develop and mature at different rates. Although all children need to be loved, some have difficulty recognizing appropriate boundaries of affection. Some children seem to have a more than average need for adult approval, attention, and affection. They often display inappropriate and aggressive physical contact with other children or adults. They are more likely to allow an adult to become too close to them and potentially allow access by a predator in exchange for attention.

2. Lack of self-confidence. An offender is looking for a child who will be a terrible witness, a child who is easily intimidated and vulnerable. This is particularly true of pedophiles who molest children over the course of several years. A child who has low self-esteem, and is overly fearful and introverted, is a much safer target than an assertive child. He is less likely to scream, and more likely to obey.

3. Children with discipline problems. Predators often choose children who have anti-social behavior and poor relationships with the adults in their lives. These children are looking elsewhere for the acceptance they are not getting from their parents and are more likely to take risks for attention. The predator is more than willing to introduce pornography, drugs, alcohol, or tobacco to lure the child. Once the child has participated in one or more illegal acts, the predator reminds him of his participation in the crimes and offers no alternative to compliance. Such children are even more vulnerable because they generally make poor witnesses, so easily are they discredited by their own anti-social behavior.

4. Children with little connection to family. One of the most important lines of defense in protecting your child is to ensure that you have open lines of communication at all times. I understand that for many reasons, this may be more difficult than you thought, but I can't stress enough how powerful it is. If your children have an adult they trust, someone they can go to when they are sad, scared, or need support, they will go to them long before it is too late. A child will alert you to people who make her feel uncomfortable, scared, or nervous. These are key triggers that, as a parent, you need to pay attention to and change. A child who has no one will be vulnerable to adults who will take advantage. She is also a better target for ongoing abuse because the predator knows that this child has no one she feels comfortable talking to, therefore she will keep their secret much longer.

5. Children who are fearful of everyone. One of my strongest arguments against teaching kids not to talk to strangers is that it inevitably causes fear of people, but more particularly the wrong people. Total strangers are not likely the ones that are going to hurt or abduct your children; it is more likely to be someone they know. Fearful children look to avoid the creepy stranger type. They have such fear and insecurity when approached by anyone that they immediately shut down their instincts and desperately search for any reason to trust the person. If the abductor is able to convince a fearful child that he is kind and can be trusted, she will be easily led away.

Overly fearful kids are easy to spot. They avoid looking directly at adults, walk with their heads down, arms crossed, jacket pulled closed. They will physically draw away from someone when spoken to and almost always follow direction without question—again, a perfect trait for a target.

Warning Signs: Access

Most children are lured away easily and without the need for violence. However, there are cases in which a child is attacked, seemingly out of the blue. The abductor will violently grab, drag, or push a child into a vehicle, alleyway, or building to complete the abduction. This is called a blitz attack.

These types of attacks seem to generate the most amount of media attention because they are so violent and frightening from the start. However, the blitz attack is not the most common choice of abductors, since it is very risky. A child may scream, fight, and draw attention to himself, putting the predator at great risk of detection and capture.

An abductor who resorts to a blitz attack has doubts about his communication skills; he knows he is not likely to succeed in luring a child away. He therefore relies on his size and strength to gain instant control over the much smaller child and to instill immediate fear to make the child comply.

The abductor is most scared of getting caught, so time is valuable to him. He needs the child to cooperate completely, or his plan will likely be ruined. He will use threats of violence or weapons to further convince a child that he means business. The mere fact that he needs these tools is a sign that he is vulnerable and knows the risk of getting caught.

Unfortunately, many children who are victims of a blitz attack are so shocked and frightened that they freeze and follow the abductor's orders instead of screaming and fighting for their lives. Still, it is important for a child to be told that if she is a victim of a blitz attack, she must draw as much attention to herself as possible. This includes kicking, screaming, biting, poking, jabbing—anything that it takes to get away or direct others to come to her aid.

Kids should always scream whatever comes to their minds. They don't need to be taught, as some safety advocates suggest, to scream "this is not my parent" or "fire." Anyone who has a child knows that there is a distinctive, blood-curdling sound that comes from a terrified child. If a child is fighting for his life and screaming, you can trust that passersby will understand that it is serious. Give your child permission, right now, to do anything it takes to get away from a person who is trying to move him against his will.

Here's an example of how a child's response can positively determine the outcome of a blitz attack.

In October 2004, a ten-year-old girl was walking down a residential street in Toronto, Ontario. She was approached by a male who grabbed her by the arm and tried to convince her to go with him. This brave, smart young girl refused and tried to walk around him. When he then attempted to fondle her, she screamed, kicked him, and ran for safety. The offender quickly fled. He got away—but so did she.

The papers reminded parents to be on the lookout, and to have their children walk in groups whenever possible, since the predator was still at large. Although it was necessary to warn the community of this potential risk, such reports can inflate the fear and paranoia that many parents already harbor. The message can quickly be reduced to a fear-induced oversimplification: "Don't let your kids out."

Many people would call that little girl lucky. I would say that luck had little to do with it (other than that she was unlucky to have crossed paths with the predator in the first place). This case could have had a tragic outcome, but it didn't. It was still very frightening to the child, parents, and community, but it is also very empowering. Remember, she got away!

Unfortunately, she did not see the man before it was too late, but given the circumstances she did the right thing in screaming and drawing as much attention to herself as she could. Instead of being afraid of letting her out alone again, her parents should feel better about her safety. Her skills were tested, and she passed. They should discuss what happened right before the man grabbed her arm and how she felt when she first saw him. Did he make her uncomfortable? What could she have done that would have helped avoid his getting close enough to grab her by the arm? Remind her to trust her instincts.

This incident has a happy ending, and a happy consequence as well: the girl's parents will know that if their daughter is faced with a similar threat, she will know what to do. That is, as long as she is praised for her actions and the focus does not turn into fear.

Take note when your children make safe choices. Praise them. Focus on the actions of your children and not the offender. Point out what they did right in the situation. Give them permission to do it again if necessary. Acknowledge the danger that your children may have faced, but credit their actions. You will find that this will reduce your fear for your child's safety, and increase his confidence in making safe choices.

All children will eventually feel the need to gain more independence from their parents. This is perfectly natural. A problem usually arises because the parent is not ready at the same time. It is important to test your kids and their knowledge and reactions. This does not mean that every child needs to have an encounter with a predator before you will know if he will be safe. You can talk about realistic scenarios with your kids. Ask them what they would do if they were in the same situation. Use the example above. Learn from their reactions.

AMBER Alert

When a child is abducted, time is critical. The faster a report is made to the police, the greater the chance of the child being recovered safely. Saving a child who has been abducted depends on the speed in which the police and community react.

The statistics are alarming, but important to know. In nonparental abductions, 44 percent of children are murdered within the first hour of abduction. That number increases to 72 percent within three hours. Of all abducted children, 91 percent will not survive beyond twenty-four hours.

The AMBER Alert was established in the United States in 1996, after the tragic kidnapping and murder of a nine-year-old girl named Amber Hagerman. Amber was kidnapped while riding her bicycle near her home in Arlington, Texas, and subsequently murdered.

It was a disturbing, brutal case that caused law enforcement, broadcast media, and the community to get together to devise a program that would allow the sharing of vital information in high-risk abduction cases.

AMBER stands for America's Missing Broadcast Emergency Response, and is based on the premise that by using television, radio, and all forms of media including electronic highway signs, which can post a fleeing vehicle description to motorists, an abductor may be located more quickly and result in saving an abducted child's life. Although the system is American, the AMBER Alert is also used across Canada.

The AMBER Alert system is meant to make people pay close attention to the details of every single case—for this reason, many cities are careful not to overuse it, which could desensitize the community. There are specific requirements before law enforcement can use the AMBER Alert.

- The abducted child must be under eighteen years of age.
- There must be confirmation that she/he has been abducted.
- Police must have sufficient information to make a search for the child possible, such as a description of the child, abductor, accomplices, the suspect's vehicle, etc.
- Police must determine that the child is in *serious* danger—in other words, in a life-threatening situation.

The AMBER Alert has rarely been used in Canada. This is because child abductions that meet the above criteria are very rare. The most common child abductions are parental abductions, almost none of which meet the AMBER Alert criteria. While parental abductions are serious and criminal, a child's life is not usually at risk when a parent is the abductor.

Parental Abduction

In a perfect world, children would be safe from all harm, vengeance, and tragedy. In a perfect world, there would be no abduction. But in today's world, when almost one out of two marriages ends in separation or divorce, the issue of child custody and access often becomes a point of bitter conflict. If the parents cannot come to a mutual agreement, the best interests of the children may not be served. Anger, disappointment, grief, frustration, vengeance, and finally, retaliation may occur. Hundreds of times every year in Canada, retaliation takes the form of a child being abducted.

Parental abduction is the most common type of child abduction in North America. On average, 400 children are victims of parental abduction in Canada each year, in comparison with 350,000 cases per year in the United States. In 2001 there were 387 cases of parental abduction in Canada. That is almost seventy-seven times more than the five true stranger abductions reported that same year. It is obvious that children are at much greater risk of being abducted by a parent than by a stranger or even an acquaintance.

Although the risks are greater, you have the ability to prevent such a loss. As in non-parental abductions, there are warning signs, profiles, and specific things that you can do to keep your kids safe.

Let's look at some facts. You do not necessarily have to be a non-custodial parent in order to abduct. Even if you have custody of your child, and your ex-partner has legal visitation rights only, if you take the child away without telling anyone where you are, and with the intention to deprive the other parent of access, you have abducted your child.

Abduction in contravention of a custody order occurs when a parent, whether or not he or she has lawful care of a child under fourteen years old, unlawfully removes them and deprives the other parent of the child. So legal custody does not necessarily allow someone the complete and sole right of access to a child. This is important to understand, especially if you are a non-custodial parent who has legal rights to see your child, or a full-custody parent who does not wish to allow access to the children.

Who tends to abduct their kids more, mothers or fathers? Actually, the numbers are just about even. A mother is more likely to abduct her child after a court order has been made, and will often keep the child longer than the father. A father will tend to abduct shortly before a court date, and turn the children over to authorities sooner than the mother.

Most children abducted by their parents are between the ages of three and seven, and the split is equal between boys and girls. Most children are abducted from home rather than school or a public area, and violence is not typically a factor.

The good news is that the majority of parental abductions do not last more than seven days, and there is almost always contact between the abductor and the searching parent.

Prevention, as in every issue of child safety, is the key. To protect your children from parental abduction, you should take the following steps.

- Legally and formally establish custody and visitation of the children. Make sure that this is legally enforceable by stating that any police officer has authority to act in the event of breach of the agreement. If you do not specifically name the police, unless it is a clear abduction, the police may not have the authority to act. They will have no choice but to suggest that you seek civil action.
- If there is a concern of abduction, or if there is a history of abuse or family violence, request the courts to grant supervised access only. This will allow your children to visit their other parent, but under controlled, supervised situations.
- Never allow the non-custodial parent to have access to the child's passport, visa, social insurance number, or birth certificate. This could aid him or her in transporting the child out of the country. If you feel that your child is at risk of parental abduction, do not permit him to travel with the other parent for any reason. This way, you will not be forced to turn over these important documents.
- Include in the custody order a provision that prohibits any school authority, daycare centres, or babysitters from releasing your child to the non-custodial parent without your consent.

The risk of abduction may increase at specific times of the year, such as Christmas and summer school breaks. It also increases when there are upcoming court dates, or if custody has recently been awarded to one parent (and lost by the other) through a court decision. These situations may increase the risk of parental abduction and you will need to be aware of the warning signs that plans may be in the works.

Some warning signs may include

- your ex-partner's requests to take the children on a vacation out of town
- an unexplained change of attitude in your ex-partner, either becoming angrier and more confrontational, or suddenly becoming friendly and cooperative
- the children have been asked to keep secrets from you
- sudden arrival of family members from out of town or another country
- your ex-partner's recent job resignation, home sale, bank account closure, or other apparent preparation to leave town

It is important to keep your situation in perspective and understand that any one of these indicators, on its own, may be insignificant and mean nothing. However, if several of these warning signs are consistent with your situation, you need to protect your children by taking the following steps.

- Notify the police immediately to intervene and make a report.
- Teach your children to never go anywhere with anyone without your personal permission. *This must include the other parent.*
- Teach your child her phone number (with area code), your full name, and how to make a collect call.
- Teach your child that he should question anyone who reports that you have suddenly died or been injured.
- Ensure that everyone who cares for your child, including schools, daycares, babysitters, family, neighbors, and friends, are aware of your custody agreement. Submit a copy of the order to schools and daycares.
- Keep a list of information that may help the police find the non-custodial parent if needed. Record his or her vehicle type, license plate number, addresses and phone numbers of his or her friends and family in and out of town. Keep a recent photograph handy.

- Demand that your school call you immediately if your child is ever absent from class.
- Ensure that you notify the school personally if your child will be absent and give a reason for the absence.

Abduction is indeed a parent's worst nightmare. However, it doesn't have to be. Children are hurt by people they know more often than by complete strangers. You have control over their safety. It is the predators among us that we must be wary of. Predators—like the pedophile.

Chapter Five

Pedophiles:
Masters of Manipulation

I am a mother of three girls, and I worry all the time about them being sexually assaulted. I was abused by my uncle, first when I was eight, and again when I was ten. He did not live close by, so it did not happen all the time, but every time he came to visit I would lock myself in the bathroom. Sometimes I would vomit from the fear and disgust. I have never told the police. I haven't told anyone. He is still alive and lives in a small community in Ontario. Is it possible that he has been cured of being a pedophile?

Pedophiles, child molesters, sexual deviants, abusers. These are all terms commonly used to describe those who commit one of the most unspeakable crimes. For most people, the images evoked by the word *pedophile* are too repulsive to dwell on. From my experience as a police officer who investigated such crimes, I can appreciate your reluctance to look deeply into this disturbing and all too common deviancy.

The Straight Goods on Pedophiles
Let me begin by setting the record straight with some facts about this uncomfortable topic.

1. Pedophilia is not a disease and therefore can't be "cured."
It is a sexual desire for and attraction to children. You are not going to convince a heterosexual man to suddenly be attracted to another

man, regardless of the amount of therapy involved. The same goes for a pedophile. You will not persuade a pedophile to stop being sexually attracted to children. Although pedophiles are commonly involved in adult sexual relationships, they often use them as fronts to gain access to their main targets: children.

2. A pedophile may never become a child molester.
A person may fantasize throughout his entire life about engaging in sex with a child, but may never act on those fantasies. He will still be a pedophile, but never cross the line and become a child molester. However, the vast majority of pedophiles do end up crossing the line, either by possessing images of child sexual abuse or directly molesting children. Some child molesters will leave hundreds of victims in their wake.

3. All child molesters are not necessarily pedophiles.
A child molester is someone who has sexually molested a child. This criminal may have molested only one child in his life, and done so out of opportunity, curiosity, anger, or for some reason other than having a preferred sexual attraction to children. It is not correct to label all child molesters as pedophiles.

4. It is not illegal to be a pedophile.
Everyone is free to fantasize about whatever they choose. A pedophile has a sexual attraction to children, and the feeling in itself is not illegal. However, it is illegal to be a child molester.

5. Over 90 percent of pedophiles are men.
Although women do account for a small percentage of pedophiles, the vast majority are men. Women who sexually abuse children often do this in partnership with a man. They may also victimize their own children, or other children in their care.

6. A pedophile can be anyone.
A pedophile may live in your neighborhood, work next to you,

attend your church, coach your child's hockey team, work as a security guard or a lawyer, be your child's teacher, doctor, or dentist. He can be rich, poor, smart, or foolish, but he is almost always the "nice guy" in town.

7. A pedophile is a master of manipulation.

A pedophile is driven by his sexual desire to control, seduce, and engage in sexual acts with children. If he is to be successful in luring, grooming, and eventually abusing a child, he needs to be seen as a kind, warm, giving man. He needs to make children and their parents trust him and he has sophisticated methods of achieving this. Some convicted pedophiles have confessed to molesting hundreds of children before ever being detected.

8. A pedophile is easier to spot than you may think.

Pedophiles seem to have consistent and common characteristics. Their pattern of behavior is not only predictable but can be easily detected if you know what to look for. (Later in this chapter I will talk further about the warning signs.)

How Many Pedophiles Are There?

It is impossible to estimate how many pedophiles there are in Canada, the U.S., or worldwide, because many of them appear to live normal everyday lives and they work hard at keeping their deviant fantasies secret. Often the media will blend the terms *pedophile* and *child molester* when talking about a case of child molestation. This can lead one to believe that all pedophiles are actively molesting children.

In fact, there are many, many people who have sexual urges toward children, but we remain unaware of their urges because they indulge them privately, usually through erotica and photographs that they collect. Many of them will eventually act out their fantasies by seeking a target and sexually molesting him or her.

Pedophiles have a sexual preference for children, and are often called *preferential child molesters*. This simply means that they choose children (usually under the age of thirteen) not merely because an opportunity presents itself but because they are actually sexually aroused by them. One characteristic that makes pedophiles so dangerous is their potential to molest very large numbers of children over their lifetimes. Although, like an abductor, they will have a preferred age and gender for their targets, they also tend to desire frequency and variety in their victims. This is why there are often several prior victims that come forward when a pedophile is captured.

Pedophiles may use a variety of methods to control and ultimately abuse children. They will go where children are, or where they will have authority over them. That is why you will find that captured pedophiles worked as teachers, coaches, child care workers, clergymen, or camp counselors. A pedophile may even begin relationships with single mothers simply to gain access to their children.

Typically pedophiles keep to themselves; however, there are highly organized groups with international memberships. Some members of organizations such as the North American Man-Boy Love Association (NAMBLA), or the Rene Guyon Society, actually believe that adults can have healthy and harmless sexual relationships with children. These groups lobby (unsuccessfully, thank goodness) to decriminalize sexual assault of children. What makes these groups dangerous, other than their obvious intent on continuously victimizing children, is that they actively seek to expose law enforcement stings and frustrate attempts to capture child molesters. The Internet has assisted pedophiles in more ways than we could ever have imagined. Not only are they able to exchange images of child sexual abuse, and tips on how to lure their victims, they now have access to victims they otherwise would never have reached. (I'll discuss Internet safety issues in chapter six.)

All pedophiles are a risk to your child's safety, regardless of whether they fantasize only, act individually, or act as part of an organization. Their focus is always on gaining access to children and they have the potential to act upon their fantasies at any time. It is vital that you consider the people in your environment, and take the precautions necessary to ensure that your child is kept safe from these deviants.

A "Special" Case: Female Pedophiles

The vast majority of pedophiles are men. But there are female sex offenders and child molesters. There are important differences in the way that women will molest children, but the harm they do is no less scarring to the victim. Often, when women sex offenders are caught, and even when they are convicted of having sexual contact with children, they describe this contact as a loving relationship.

The most famous female sex offender in American history is a Seattle schoolteacher named Mary Kay Letourneau. At thirty-four, Letourneau was convicted of two counts of second-degree child rape (as it is described by U.S. law) of a seventh-grade student, and sentenced to seven-and-a-half years in prison. Letourneau was twenty-seven when she first met the victim, who was then a student in her grade two class. Five years later, when the student was thirteen, Letourneau was again his teacher. She had sex with the boy and became pregnant.

Letourneau was given a light sentence but told not to contact the fourteen-year-old victim, a condition that she quickly breached. She then returned to prison to serve her sentence.

This case caused controversy in the United States and in Canada. People were torn about how to view it: was it a simple case of child molestation, or a love story, as the accused wants people to believe? Letourneau was released in August 2004, and married her victim in 2005. They have two children together.

It is alarming to think that Letourneau's point of view did gain some measure of acceptance among the general public. It seems that because there was no violence involved, and because the accused is a small, attractive, educated female, the severity of the offense was minimized. Indeed, some people believed that no offense had taken place. Yet I expect that if the accused were a thirty-four-year-old man who seduced and impregnated a thirteen-year-old girl, most observers would be sickened by the act and would not hesitate to call it abuse.

A case like Letourneau's is not common, but her profile is typical for a female sex offender. Women who commit sexual offenses against children often do so by developing a strong attachment and often believe that "love" is what motivates and explains their actions, often similar to a pedophile who believes that he has the best interest of a child at heart.

But these are not the only type of female sex offenders. Some females will work with a male counterpart by helping him to gain access to children. These women will often be abused and controlled by their partners and fear for their own safety. This is usually paired with a strong fear of abandonment.

Women who sexually abuse their own children are often immature and have extreme fears of rejection and abandonment. If the woman has been abandoned by her spouse, she may use her child as an emotional and sexual substitute. Women who abuse their own children may even do so out of anger and resentment, and commonly have very serious psychological and emotional problems.

Even though anomalies do exist, it is rare for a female sex offender to fit the profile of a preferential sex offender (pedophile).

The Warning Signs

Preferential child molesters, pedophiles, have distinct patterns of behavior that are highly predictable. As a parent, you must learn to identify these patterns as warning signs, as they are extremely valuable tools in assessing whether someone represents a risk to your children. Each one of these characteristics, taken on its own, can mean little, but if you can identify a large number of them in an individual you know, you need to remove that person from your child's environment and never allow him to have unsupervised access.

A pedophile is someone who

1. Shows an intense interest in children and childlike things

It is hard not to care about kids. In fact, you may be suspicious of those who show no interest in children at all. However, there is a balance between average or appropriate interest, and excessive interest. Pedophiles will find everything about your child interesting, seem to relate to her better than adults do, and prefer her company.

2. Has idealistic views of children

A pedophile may refer to children as pure and innocent, and put them on a pedestal. They may think of children as "projects," offering them extra help after school, for instance, or arranging meetings with the child for ostensibly good and honest reasons. They will likely invest a great deal of time and effort in one child, rather than offering equal attention to an entire group of kids. Some pedophiles have a belief that they are looking out for and have genuine love for children.

3. Has limited peer relationships

Pedophiles feel more comfortable around children. They do not often associate with peers in their age group. They would much prefer to sit at the "children's table" at a dinner party than with the adults.

4. Calls children "friends"

Pedophiles will surround themselves with childlike things that attract children and encourage friendships. A pedophile will often be the "cool older guy" in town, and you may find that many kids hang out at his house. He will attract kids with his lack of rules and defiance of parental controls.

5. Is over twenty-five years old, single, never married, lives alone or with parents

Just because someone matches this description does not mean he is a pedophile. However, if he meets several other criteria listed here, you should be seeing this as a warning sign.

6. Moves often and unexpectedly

Often pedophiles will feel they have "worn out their welcome" in a particular community, or feel they are close to getting caught. They will move regularly to avoid detection or confrontation from suspecting parents, or to find a new pool of victims.

7. Participates in and organizes activities that exclude other adults

For obvious reasons, a pedophile needs access and privacy to commit the abuse. He will avoid inviting other adults to planned events or outings.

8. Takes numerous photographs of children

Pedophiles collect photographs, mementoes, symbols, and anything else from their victims and/or other targets that might enhance their fantasies. Most notably, they take an inappropriate number of pictures or videos of children, in their communities, at events, or simply when playing. The pedophile may also have a lot of child-focused movies or music CDs, more than seems appropriate for a single man to possess. These are used for fantasy as well as to lure children into their homes.

9. Works and plays in areas that attract children

Pedophiles typically choose work environments that allow access to children. This may include working in a school (as a teacher or in some other capacity) or daycare, as a coach or volunteer in a community centre, or in any other profession that is child focused.

10. Decorates his home with childlike décor

A pedophile is constantly trying to attract children, and relates to them better than to adults. His home, dress, and demeanor will often reflect childlike characteristics.

11. Is generous with gifts

Many pedophiles choose targets that are needy—both for material things and for attention. They are quick to provide a needy child with toys, games, and money to lure him into a position of trust and eventually a sense of indebtedness.

How a Pedophile Targets and Lures His Victims

Pedophiles prefer to be around children rather than adults. This does not mean that everyone who loves children is potentially a pedophile. Adults who work with children and spend a great deal of time with kids, even though they may enjoy their work, sometimes reach a point when they think, "I really need to spend some time with adults." New parents especially can likely relate to this desire to talk about anything but the baby for a few hours! Pedophiles, on the other hand, will do everything they can to avoid being in the exclusive company of adults.

Pedophiles generally fall within two categories: introverted/immature, and seductive. They display different patterns of behavior and different methods of luring children, but both are dangerous and you should learn to recognize them.

1. Introverted/Immature. Many pedophiles who are introverted and immature have patterns of behavior that clearly show their lack of sophistication when it comes to communication. Without the conversational skills to successfully seduce and lure children into abuse, they have no option but to molest strangers or very young children.

You will find an introverted, immature pedophile hanging around parks and playgrounds and other areas that children frequent. He may be a "flasher" and expose himself to children, or engage in inappropriate sexual conversation. If he continues to have difficulty gaining access to children, he may either marry a woman who already has children, or have children of his own whom he will molest from an early age.

2. Seductive. A seductive pedophile is a master manipulator. He is a deviant who is able to not only persuade children to trust him but many times also the parents and other family members. He will carefully select his targets and begin to seduce them by offering gifts, money, and attention. He will work patiently, sometimes over long periods of time, to gain the child's trust and lower her sexual inhibitions. He will gradually introduce pornography and touching until the child is less frightened and more willing to trade sex for the gifts or attention she has come to need.

A seductive pedophile will often have many victims within the same neighborhood, sports team, or club, and maintain the abusive relationships simultaneously without any detection. He is usually in a position of authority and spends a great deal of time learning about and listening to his targets. He makes the time to get to know kids. He invests the time to choose victims who will not only allow him to continue the abuse, but can be manipulated into believing that they *must* continue.

One of the problems that seductive pedophiles encounter is breaking off the abuse when they are no longer attracted to the child because he or she has become too old to satisfy the pedophile's tastes. Many cases of long-term child abuse come to light only after the pedophile has resorted to violence and threats to turn the child away.

I worked on a case that, to this day, affects the way I view pedophiles and the power they have over their victims and their families.

There was a sixty-five-year-old man living in a small community. He seemed, to everyone who met him, a great guy. Families in the neighborhood described him as the typical "grandpa type."

A divorced man—I'll call him John—he now lived alone in a three-story walk-up bordering on a lower-income housing project bursting with kids. He was always neat and clean in his appearance, and he spent many hours sitting on his patio watching the children playing in the street. He had two little dogs that the kids loved. John made a point of taking them for their walk along the street and past the local elementary school during lunch hour and after school every day. The children and the school officials all knew him.

John was a generous man. He understood that the children in this neighborhood had little spending money and often went without. Although he was not rich, he was able to give the children a few dollars here and there so they could buy some candy for themselves. On occasion, he would even slip the single mothers a few dollars to help them get by.

He took the time to meet all the parents and participated in block barbecues and get-togethers. He was a real member of this little community and many people called him Gramps. No one had a bad thing to say about him and he was invited to many homes for dinner on more than one occasion.

John was also an avid photographer. He didn't have a fancy camera, just a 35 mm and an older VHS video camera, but he took great pictures. He loved to take photographs of the children playing in the sprinklers during the summer, and often displayed them in frames around his apartment.

Jenna was ten years old, with long, straight brown hair and a huge smile. John saw her outside playing one afternoon and was struck by how pretty she was.

He later saw her walking her dog alone in a nearby park. She stopped to talk to him and pet his two tiny dogs. He seemed very nice. When John asked if he could take her picture, Jenna was surprised, but she agreed and posed for him sitting on a rock in front of a lake.

After that, John spent a lot more time outside his apartment building, hoping to see Jenna walking her dog or playing. He was lucky, because she loved to be outside and was often unsupervised. John introduced Jenna to some other children in the neighborhood, children who had been over to his apartment many times in the past. The other children told Jenna what a great guy John was, and how he would give them money and presents for no reason at all. Jenna liked John too, even though she thought he took too many pictures of her.

One afternoon, John invited Jenna up to his apartment for some ice cream and to watch a Disney movie. Jenna agreed, and, without asking her parents, went to John's. She couldn't believe how many Disney movies he had! She looked through his movie collection while he got her ice cream, and she saw a couple of movies with covers of people having sex. They made her feel uncomfortable. John told her that was perfectly natural, and that they didn't have to watch them if she didn't want to. She was relieved. They spent that afternoon watching movies and laughing. Jenna liked John. He seemed very nice to her and she agreed to visit him again. He gave her a kiss on the cheek when she left, which she didn't mind.

Jenna returned to John's apartment several times that summer, often watching movies and eating ice cream. Her parents were not aware of her new "friend," since John had asked her to keep it a secret. Sometimes John would talk to her about sex and women, which made her uneasy, but she was starting to get used to it. One day, John told her that he was making a movie for a friend and he thought she would be a great actress. Jenna was thrilled when John asked her to be in his movie. She agreed happily and enjoyed dancing around the living room to music while John took videos. John explained that it would be fun if she would take her clothes off when she danced.

It is not important to explain what transpired next, except to say that John was a pedophile and had previous convictions of making child pornography in a nearby city.

The process of seduction had taken John almost two months, but to him, Jenna was worth it. She was John's ideal target—a ten-year-old female. After John was arrested, I asked him, "What age would you consider to be too young for you, John?" He answered quite simply, "Anything under ten would be disgusting."

You see, pedophiles have limits themselves. They have guidelines and preferences and choices. John was a preferential child molester, a pedophile. Jenna was neither his first victim nor his last. He married a woman thirty years his junior, and from the wedding pictures I saw, she looked like a little girl herself. John had a family who lived in another province, but it was obvious from the videos I viewed of their family get-togethers that they did not feel comfortable around him.

John was charged and pled guilty to four counts of sexual interference with a child under fourteen. He did not spend more than one day in jail—the day I put him there while I was processing the charge—and that puts shame on the judge who sentenced him. To this day, if John is still alive, he is seventy-five, and almost certainly preying on another community somewhere in Canada.

I searched everywhere for John's "collection," but never found it, which saddens me. To a pedophile, his collection of pornography and erotica is his most valued possession. It would have been rewarding to take from him something that meant so much.

The Collection

Almost all pedophiles will have a collection of pornography or erotica that they accumulate over a lifetime of fantasies and abuse. A man doesn't just become a pedophile—he has always been a pedophile. From a fairly early age, he will begin to collect books, magazines, movies, pictures, drawings, diaries, clothing, sexual aids, souvenirs, and any other item he can use to aid in his recollection of past encounters, or future fantasies. Not all pedophiles collect all of these items, and collections vary in size. What they have in common is that they are the pedophile's most cherished possession. Some pedophiles are known to bury their collection to avoid detection, or keep a secret storage space to protect it.

Collections are key in detecting if someone is a pedophile. It seems that the richer, older, and more private the pedophile, the larger the collection. Pedophiles can collect, reproduce and store their erotica or pornography on discs, Palm Pilots, and tapes. They may find images of young children in a Zellers catalog stimulating and painstakingly cut out each image to add to their collection. This to a pedophile may be erotica. A collection will almost always have child pornography, which in itself is one of the fastest-growing crimes against children in the world.

Child Sexual Abuse Images (Child Pornography)

There are many terms thrown around to describe this particularly horrible crime against children. Some call it kiddie porn, others call it child pornography. The correct term is *child sexual abuse images*, because that is what they are. The term *pornography* lends an air of legitimacy that has been established by the purveyors of adult pornography such as Larry Flynt of *Hustler* magazine fame. But there is a big difference: those who participate in making adult pornography do so voluntarily; children never have a choice. They are victimized, lured, and abused. To call child sexual abuse images "pornography" is a misrepresentation of what it really is—a crime.

Thanks to the Internet, the market for child sexual abuse images has increased exponentially. Out of one home in Toronto, police seized more than 1 million images. The largest case in British Columbia yielded 30,000 images of child sexual abuse from one pedophile.

In Canada it is a crime to possess, make, print, publish, transmit, make available, distribute, sell, import, export, or possess for the purpose of transmission any child sexual abuse images. It is also a crime to simply access and view these images, or to transmit them to yourself.

This law has some teeth, thank goodness. Here is an example.

If you were to go on the Internet and key in child pornography on a search engine, looking for child sexual abuse images, and one appeared, you have committed an offense and could face up to five years in prison. By simply accessing the images to view, you have contributed to the abuse.

Accessing images is only one aspect of the problem, though. Those who create the images pose the greatest threat to children. Many pornographers do not stop at photographing children in sexually explicit poses: statistics show that 44 percent of child pornographers arrested in the last three years had committed actual sexual abuse.

How many child sexual abuse images are being distributed and exchanged over the Internet? We don't know, and in fact there are likely too many to count. The Internet has launched the child pornography industry to a new level. Although laws are continually being written and revised to combat this growing concern, police around the world are constantly playing catch-up. The law can only bite if it can be applied to the offender.

What is considered a child sexual abuse image?

The law in Canada is specific when defining child pornography. Our laws apply not only to photographic images, but to drawings and writings as well. To be considered an offense, the image or writing must meet at least one of the following criteria.

- It shows a person who appears to be under eighteen years old engaged in or depicted as engaged in explicit sexual activity.
- The dominant characteristic of the image or depiction is for a sexual purpose.
- It depicts a sexual organ or anal region of a person under eighteen years old.
- The written material or visual representation encourages sexual activity with a person under eighteen years. This can include any drawings, paintings, prints, sculptures, or computer graphics, or any non-textual representation that can be perceived visually.

If an image is created for a sexual purpose, depicting a child who appears to be under eighteen engaging in sexual activity (regardless of whether they really are eighteen) it is a crime—not "art"—period. Although there have been cases where pedophiles were charged with possession of child pornography, and have defended their rights using claims of artistic merit, or educational, scientific, or medical purposes, this is still, thank goodness, a crime. However, change did come to the law when the Supreme Court of British Columbia ruled that it was lawful for someone to create writings depicting sexual acts with children as long as it was for their own use and never shared or transmitted.

A simple nude photograph of a child is not considered an image of child sexual abuse—unless the dominant characteristic is sexual, or the child is engaged in a sexual act, or it shows close images of sexual organs. If a child is standing nude, or sitting in a bathtub, you do not necessarily have images of child sexual abuse. If you have nude baby pictures of your children, you do not likely have child pornography.

The law recognizes two categories of child sexual abuse images: commercial and homemade. Commercial images are produced for the purpose of sale or exchange through commercial means. It is illegal not only to possess images of child sexual abuse but also to buy and sell them. Therefore, many images are imported from outside countries and sources. Commercial child sexual abuse images are much more available in foreign countries, but buyers are most frequently from the U.S. and Canada.

Homemade images are typically better in quality and are usually not made for use or sale through commercial venues. Homemade images of child sexual abuse are routinely swapped among pedophiles. Child victims who are in these images are not likely abducted and used for the purposes of creating this form of pornography, but rather persuaded to pose for each picture by pedophiles who have seduced them.

Why do pedophiles collect images of child sexual abuse?

A pedophile collects images for several reasons, besides the obvious that it assists in his sexual arousal and fantasies of engaging in sex with children. Many pedophiles use pornography to help lower a child's inhibitions, make them feel that the activity is "normal" and eventually agree to pose for pictures or videos.

Pornographers who abuse children into making these images fall into four categories.

1. Closet. This is a pedophile who does not actively or physically molest children but collects images of child sexual abuse to add to his collection. By simply having these images, he is not only committing an offense but is indirectly a child molester himself.

2. Isolated. This is a pedophile who actively molests children and routinely takes images of them for his personal use and as reminders of his victims.

3. Cottage. This is an industry run by pedophiles who exchange images of child sexual abuse for commercial purposes. These pedophiles are actively molesting the children in the images.

4. Commercial. These are pedophiles and pornographers who create images for sale to other pedophiles around the world.

What should you do if you find images of child sexual abuse?

If you find what appears to be a collection of child sexual abuse or erotica, it is essential that you call the police immediately. If you know who the images belong to, you need to speak up and alert the authorities.

Pedophiles can be anyone. Most have families and children, and appear to be pillars of the community. But pedophiles will continue to molest children for the rest of their lives unless they are stopped. The only way to stop a pedophile from abusing another child is to deny him any possible access to children. This may be accomplished through jail time, or through a court order forbidding any contact with children. It is not difficult to identify a pedophile, based on the knowledge that you now have. What can be very difficult is turning in someone whom you have loved and trusted.

You have an obligation to report any sexual abuse that you know of, including abuse from your own past. It does not matter how many years have passed; there is no statute of limitations for sexual assault cases. What matters is that the wheels are put in motion to remove a known threat from having access to any other children. Age, time, religion, sorrow, remorse—none of these can change a pedophile. Once a pedophile, always a pedophile, and a definite danger to any child he may come in contact with. Including, perhaps, your own.

National Sex Offenders Registry

On April 1, 2004, legislation to create a national registration for sex offenders in Canada received royal assent. In other words, it was finally approved after more than a year of lobbying for this very important database. The information contained in the database is controlled by the RCMP, and accessible to accredited police agencies only, not to the general public. The information assists in the investigation of crimes of a sexual nature.

A sex offender is now required to register him/herself within fifteen days of conviction or release from prison. All convicted sex offenders must submit their names, addresses, profiles, aliases, and identifying marks. Several addresses can be added to each entry, so sex offenders can be tracked from place to place. Sex offenders must re-register annually or upon each address change. They may be required to be registered for anywhere from ten years to life, depending on the sentencing of their original sex crime. If an offender fails to comply with these orders, or gives false information, there are further criminal penalties that he will face.

Here is the controversial part: the registry only has the names of sex offenders who are incarcerated, on parole, or on probation from the date that the law took effect. Sex offenders who completed their releases prior to the law coming into effect are not registered. Many predators among us are not accounted for. The National Sex Offenders Registry has been in effect in Canada since December 2004.

By establishing this national database of convicted sex offenders, our politicians are making a commitment to public safety, and our police are being given an added tool for investigating and locating potential threats in the community. Child safety advocates have been saying for years that the key to staying safe is knowledge. This database, while not perfect, is at least one step in that direction.

Chapter Six

The World Wide Web — and Those Lurking in It

The other day my sister was surfing the Net. She came across a website that said she could search for anyone on it. Out of curiosity, she keyed in my thirteen-year-old daughter's name and hit "search." She was alarmed to see that the search returned my daughter's name (including middle name), nickname, age, height, weight, address, phone number, hair and eye color, and hobbies. She called me immediately. I opened the same site and when I saw all of my daughter's information listed, I didn't know what to do. I talked to my daughter and she didn't remember filling out any forms online, but how else could all of her information be there? How can I get it removed?

As of September 2003 there were an estimated 43 million registered websites on the World Wide Web. However, even in the time it takes you to read this sentence, the total number will have changed several times.

The twenty-first century is going to take some getting used to. It doesn't seem that long ago that I was a teenager and the latest technology was the VCR. I recall cell phones as hefty as a five-pound block of cheese—and they cost more than $2,000. They were all the rage, even though you had to carry a shoulder bag that contained a heavy battery attachment. Personal computers had begun to surface but people were not really buying into the concept. My family was technologically advanced for the times: my mother had a machine called an Apple computer—every function required personal programming in DOS. She never did figure it out, even though she invested many hours in computer programming lessons. We even had a Telex machine in our home. We played our music on record players with gigantic speakers. If the record had a scratch, we would stomp a foot in the shag carpet in front of the player to get it to skip to the next cut. Our car had huge eight-track tapes that floated around the floor, crashing into glass pop bottles every time the car made a turn. I know you remember that! We researched our essays in libraries, had pen pals, five-speed bicycles, and neighbors who yelled over the fence to say hi.

We didn't have digital TV, MP3s, PlayStation, Game Boy, portable phones, TiVo, DVDs, CDs, digital movie recorders and cameras, scanners, e-mail, chat rooms, the Internet or the World Wide Web.

But no, I am not ancient! All of these changes have come within the last thirty years, most of them only within the last five or ten. Advances in technology have significantly changed everyone's life—mostly for the better. However, technology has brought a wealth of problems for parents who care about keeping their kids safe: the hazards are real, and they're serious.

One of the reasons that the online world is so dangerous for children is that kids often know more than their parents about how it works. Kids are not experts, however, at detecting danger, nor do they know how to protect themselves completely. As a result, they can be lured, tricked, and drawn into perilous situations.

It is time for parents and school officials to realize that Internet safety education needs to be as emphatic and as entrenched in schools and the home as drug and alcohol awareness. Internet safety should be part of all school curricula, at both the elementary and high school levels.

But the responsibility doesn't begin and end with your children's schools—you, the parent, are vital. And while I understand that it is difficult to find time these days for anything other than daily tasks, errands, and "life," if you are going to help protect your kids, you must find the time to learn more about the Internet. It's that simple.

If you don't, I promise you will regret it, because people around the world, with many different and often heinous motives, can get access to your children while they are sitting in the "safety" of their homes. That is, if you do nothing about it.

There are some things you can do.

1. Set clear guidelines about how the Internet can be used safely.
2. Keep the lines of communication open at all times—talk to your kids about what they're doing online.
3. Supervise their time online.

I'll discuss each of these in more detail, but first let's cover some basic information about the online world so we'll all be speaking the same language.

The Internet and the World Wide Web: The Basics

The Internet and the World Wide Web (WWW) are two different things. The Internet was invented by the United States Department of Defense in 1969 to assist in communication between military bases. "The Internet" refers to a worldwide network of inter-connected computers that use a common code to talk to each other. The World Wide Web refers to all the publicly available websites and other information sources in the world, such as newsgroups. The World Wide Web was invented in Switzerland, in 1989, by Tim Berners-Lee.

Web servers are computers that are part of the Internet. They are where websites are hosted. Computers, cell phones, or any other devices used to look at a website are also part of the Internet. A web-site is a collection of "pages" or files linked together and available over the Internet. Websites are provided by companies, organiza-tions, and individuals. A website address usually starts with "www," but that is just a standard form, and there is nothing that says that websites must start with www.

Most websites can be found by using a search engine such as

Google, Yahoo, or MSN, and in fact this is how about 90 percent of people find what they're looking for online. When you want to know more about a specific topic, you can enter key words and the search engine will return a list of websites whose encoding matches your key words. From here you can enter any website you choose. "Surfing the Net" refers to the way that users commonly navigate the Internet, by moving randomly, in a non-linear way, from one website to another.

There is no single person or organization that controls the Internet worldwide. However, there are organizations in each country that assist in formulating rules. You can usually tell where a website is from by looking at the end of the address. For example, .ca indicates Canada; .it stands for Italy; and .uk indicates the United Kingdom. The most common suffix, though, is still .com, which was originally intended for commercial sites; however, anyone can start a .com website whether a commercial venue or not. For Kidproof Canada, our web address (or URL) is www.kidproofcanada.com, even though we are Canadian.

Some countries, such as China, have filtered access, meaning that all Internet content originating from that country is screened, usually for political purposes. In most parts of the world, though, this is not the case. Our Charter of Rights and Freedoms, which is a federal statute that supersedes any other law in Canada, states that everyone has the fundamental right to freedom of thought, belief, opinion, and expression, including freedom of the press and other media of communication. This includes the Internet.

Freedom of expression is limited by criminality and the Canadian Human Rights Code. That is, as long as an expression of belief or thought does not commit an offense, or violate a human right, it is legal and permissible. Even in some criminal cases, defendants have challenged the law by saying they had the right to their beliefs and to express them. Some have actually won, because the Charter of Rights is more powerful than the Criminal Code.

Okay, this is not a book on law. What you really want to know is, Do people have the right to post anything they wish on a website?

The answer is yes—as long as it is not a form of child pornography, does not incite hatred, or commit another criminal, provincial or civil offense. Pornography, advertising, dating—most things are legal and possible on the Internet. An exception to this rule would be luring a child through the Internet for sexual or violent purposes.

What this means to parents who do not want certain websites viewed by their children is that the onus is on you, rather than on website providers or any other party, to prevent your kids from gaining access to those sites. You'll find, for instance, that some key words will give you a list of images, websites, and "pop-ups" (small advertisements that pop up on your screen) that may not be appropriate for your child to view.

Filtering software

Filtering software works as a layer of protection, but it should not be thought of as a replacement for personal supervision. Many filtering software programs keep a large portion of unwanted materials out, but no program keeps it all out. Kids, especially very computer-savvy kids, can disable the software if they choose. Filtering software tends to be more useful for younger children, since they are not usually looking for a variety of information. A teenager, however, may need to research a history assignment, for instance, and most filtering software will cut out a huge number of sites based on a wide range of key words or images.

You may find that filtering software becomes more of a hassle than a help as your kids get older. However, there are new products being developed that offer varying degrees of access, supervision, and control. (I'll cover the use of this and other technologies to protect kids in chapter ten.)

While the police in many countries are doing their best to prevent pedophiles and other predators from using the Internet to lure their victims, it is an uphill battle, to say the least, and many predators avoid detection.

Privacy and the Net

Personal information is sought by various parties through the Internet. Aggressive marketing firms use the information they gather so that their expensive marketing campaigns will hit the bull's-eye— your kids and their disposable income. These marketing research machines constantly encourage online surveys, interactive games, and giveaways to gain valuable feedback from kids about what interests them, as well as direct access to their e-mail inbox.

Industry guidelines in Canada that pertain to the collection, transfer, and request of personal information for kids under thirteen lie with the Canadian Marketing Association. But these are just guidelines, and following them is strictly voluntary.

There are far stronger regulations in place in the United States. This is good, because some of the biggest and most popular websites visited by Canadian kids are American sites. In the U.S., commercial websites are prohibited from gathering information about children under the age of thirteen without giving them clear notice of how they gather and use the information. They must also obtain parental consent. However, keep in mind that a child can easily fill in the blanks on a form and pretend to be you! Again, nothing beats clear guidelines, parental supervision, and open communication while online.

Why is it so problematic if your child gives out personal information? Well, the information that any one of us provides online can, and often does, find its way into the hands of others, whose purposes may be much more insidious than the marketers'. I'm talking, of course, about predators.

If you find that information about your child has been posted on a website, or if your child is being harassed through online message boards, you can contact your local Internet service provider (often known as an ISP; examples are Sympatico, Rogers, AOL, and Shaw) and request help to find the host of the website that is publishing the information. You may then contact the Internet provider of the offending site and alert it to your concerns. If the reported host is breaking any rules of its contract with the ISP, the service provider can request removal of the offending information or threaten shutting down the site. If the ISP determines that there may be a criminal offense committed, it may contact the police or suggest you do so.

What Are Kids Doing Online?

Kids use the Internet not only as a means of communication but for entertainment. Kids are participating in chat rooms, instant messaging to other friends, entering contests, downloading music, sharing music files, playing games, filling out surveys to get free products, or watching movies.

Kids use the Internet to

- chat with friends over instant messaging (IM). This is often called "MSNing," after the most popular IM provider.
- meet new people and chat in chat rooms
- surf the Net for school research or areas of personal interest
- send and receive e-mail
- share files with others (often music, movies, or other pirated materials)
- fill out online surveys to win or receive free products
- enter online contests
- play games (single or multi-user)
- shop

Many of these things are well intentioned and quite enjoyable. However, each one has the potential to pose a risk to your child.

Instant messaging, chat rooms, and text messaging

Kids rarely use the telephone these days—which, for the most part, is an agreeable change! The most popular way for kids to "talk" to their friends is through instant messaging (IM). IM allows people to talk to each other in real time through the Internet. There are different programs available for kids to choose from, such as ICQ (a clever short form for "I seek you") and IRC (Internet Relay Chat), but by far the most popular instant messaging service is MSN Messenger. It requires the user to download the free software from the website, sign up for a free Hotmail e-mail account, and then, presto—instant messaging. IM can be used in any country that has access to the Internet, so it is a great way to communicate with friends and family without incurring long-distance phone charges.

IM services can be set up by kids so that outside users are blocked from accessing or joining their conversations. Kids compile a list of "approved" e-mail addresses, usually their friends'. Because it is more controlled than chat rooms, IM is much safer. However, there are still risks involved. Kids may allow someone they don't really know onto their approved lists, and often they enter as "friends of friends." Popularity is judged by how many friends are on their lists and kids will often allow strangers on to bolster their prestige.

The other risk to using IM is that most programs, including MSN Messenger, have a feature that allows users to post a personal profile. This is designed to capture some personal information, including name, hobbies, and likes and dislikes, which are intended to bring together people with shared interests. Some programs such as www.nexopia.com (a predominantly Canadian IM and chat service) allow users to post digital pictures for others to see. If your child fills out a personal profile, it is available for anyone on the Internet. If he posts his photo, not only is he elevating the risk of unwanted solicitations, he is also increasing the risk of his photos being used in pornographic materials by morphing. (Morphing is when an image is altered and blended with another image to give the illusion that the picture is real.) Make it clear to your kids that they should never fill out personal profiles online or post their picture.

If your child is using instant messaging, he or she is at risk—it's that simple. But the presence of risk does not mean you should prohibit the activity entirely. What parents need to do is understand how IM works, and set clear rules and guidelines surrounding its use both in their homes and through any other Internet access their children have.

If you are not sure how it works, sign up yourself and give it a try, even join a chat room. Or, better yet, have your kids show you how it works. They will love the opportunity to show you their skills, and you can also make use of this time to talk to them about safety.

Chat rooms are much more risky. These are areas, or "rooms," on the Web that you can enter to talk to or meet people from anywhere in the world. Chat rooms attract predators and other inappropriate chatters who may pose a risk to your child. An IM user can be invited into a private chat room, where other users can be blocked. Often if a predator has found a child, he will continue the seduction process by inviting him into a private chat room. The use of chat rooms should be strictly prohibited by you.

Text messaging (or SMS, which stands for short message system) is another way to communicate through cell phones. It has begun to peak in popularity because of the number of kids who carry them. It is usually less expensive than making a phone call, and instead of making five different phone calls to friends, the sender can reach five friends at once.

Monitoring the use of cell phones brings a new set of problems for parents, especially when text messaging is going on. Kids have their cell phones with them at all times, and they are usually on. They can receive and transmit messages wherever they are and to whomever they choose. Many cell phone plans have text messaging as a standard feature. If you are concerned that your child may be using text messaging too frequently, or receiving disturbing or harassing messages, you may ask your service provider if it can remove the text messaging feature.

Parental guidelines for safe instant messaging
- Be clear with your children: they should never fill out personal profiles, give out personal information, or post their photographs online. Make sure they understand the risks, and why you are so adamant about these rules.
- Do not allow young children to use IM. They will need to create a Hotmail e-mail account, which is difficult for you to monitor.

- Do not allow your child to enter or participate in chat rooms.
- Monitor who is on your child's approved list of contacts. Remove anyone that you do not know.

E-mail and attachments

Most parents are familiar with e-mail. It is estimated that two out of three households in Canada have a computer with access to the Internet and e-mail. Many e-mail services, such as Hotmail and Yahoo, are free, which makes it easy to set up and begin to receive e-mail messages within minutes.

E-mail is the most popular use for the Internet. Many people rarely use the Internet for anything else. It is a fast, easy, and inexpensive way to send and receive messages around the world, and most adults who use e-mail in their workplaces would agree that it's hard to imagine life without it.

Kids are using e-mail as early as six years old. In fact, preschoolers are the fastest growing segment of Internet users, according to www.bewebaware.com, a Canadian public education program on Internet safety. I highly recommend that you take the time to read through their website and learn about their very effective and positive approach to Internet safety and children. Kids, especially at the age of six, are extremely vulnerable to unwanted and disturbing messages, advertising, and scams. It is essential that you constantly monitor and supervise all Internet use while young children are online.

You should consider having a family e-mail account. This way you can monitor and block inappropriate messages that may be sent to your children. If your child has his own e-mail account, such as Hotmail, you will need his password to access it. Hotmail also allows users to set up an IM account, which is unsafe for very young people to participate in. As children get older, they naturally become more guarded with their privacy. It may be difficult to persuade your children to give you access to their e-mail accounts. To prevent this confrontation, prohibit them from creating a Hotmail account until they are older and more prepared to respond appropriately to the potential messages they will receive.

A young person's e-mail address should be guarded as carefully as his home address. Teach your kids to give their e-mail address only to friends and family who are well known to them. If you have given them permission to play an online game, but the game requires that they register with an e-mail address, make up a false e-mail address for this purpose only. Use this false address for all forms and surveys for which you do not wish to receive a reply.

Attachments are documents that are sent as part of an e-mail. They can take many forms, such as text, HTML (a page with graphics, logos, colors), or other types of specialized files that transmit photos or videos. Most parents use attachments at work to send and receive documents from other offices, customers, or co-workers. Kids, however, use attachments to send pictures or messages to other users.

Predators use attachments to send disturbing and often pornographic photos and images to children as they work toward desensitizing the child's "ick factor," which is their inner warning system that tells them that something is not right. Desensitizing is the first step in encouraging a sexual conversation. Predators may also send attachments that, when opened, infect the child's computer so that the predator can access it at any time. These attachments may contain spyware, adware, or other hijacking viruses. They can come disguised as a picture that the predator convinces the child to open. Once it is open, the predator is in. He often keeps his access a secret until it is necessary for him to reveal it to continue to control his victim. This is very frightening to a child, and a very effective display of power and intimidation. If a child begins to shut down and no longer wishes to continue with the relationship, the predator, with access to the child's computer, can easily remind the child that he has total control. He may eventually blackmail the child by threatening to send e-mail messages to others that would reveal their often sexual conversations.

Many of us receive e-mails daily that were not requested and contain a variety of advertising and often disturbing images. If you do not have anti-spam or pop-up blocker software on your computer, you should consider installing some. You can download these free over the Internet. If your child is receiving disturbing messages on her e-mail address, tell her not to respond. She should alert you to the message and you can take appropriate action by notifying the police or another reporting agency such as www.cybertip.ca.

Hackers and other computer wizards send viruses, usually through .exe or .zip files, that are designed to take over and destroy your hard drive. The world has seen powerful and widespread viruses damage thousands of networks in minutes. Teach your children never to open an attachment from anyone if you do not recognize the address, especially if it ends in .exe or .zip. And be sure to keep your anti-virus subscriptions current at all times.

Parental guidelines to safe e-mailing

- Set up a family e-mail account that contains your child's e-mail address.
- Do not allow young children to open a Hotmail account, as this will give them access to IM as well as prevent you from monitoring their messages.
- Create a false e-mail account to use for surveys and required registration fields.
- Make sure your kids know they should never open attachments from senders you do not know, or attachments that contain .exe or .zip in the subject line.
- Never respond directly to alarming or disturbing messages. Report the message to www.cybertip.ca.

Online Predators: Know Your Enemy

What is so frustrating for parents, law enforcement, and child safety advocates is that the Internet provides a temporary shield that hides the true identity of the user. The Internet opens a door to the world, meaning that your enemies can be anyone, from anywhere. It is impossible to say how many online predators there are—besides, it only takes one to get through to threaten your child's very life. It is one thing to be able to face your enemy and watch his behavior, but it is much more difficult to read between the lines of an instant message to see the clues that someone may be dangerous.

Predators on the Net are not comparable to those on the street. They actually have the advantage. Online predators lurk in chat rooms, use e-mail, instant messaging and discussion boards to solicit and seduce children. Peer-focused forums were initially designed to help teens through difficulties by using peer-to-peer contact. These forums were established with good intentions, but they create the perfect target for a predator seeking confused, lonely, and emotionally unstable teens.

Just like a pedophile who hangs out at the local park, an online predator will use the same tactics to seduce and build trust in his online targets. He will shower them with attention and understanding, support their emotions, send gifts, and be their friend. Often a predator will invest a sizable amount of time in getting to know his targets, finding and manipulating their vulnerabilities. Online predators have the advantage of anonymity. The child can easily be led to believe that he has made a new friend who is the same age and gender, when in fact his correspondent is an adult predator assuming a false identity.

Predators are constantly evaluating their targets to see if they will be easy victims. The online predator will make small, safe investments, similar to face-to-face contact, toward his targets, testing them constantly, and slowly introducing more direct solicitation. Often he will send pornographic material to help desensitize and reduce the inhibitions of the targets, eventually engaging in very explicit sexual discussions.

Most teens believe that they are Internet-savvy, but studies show this is not the case. Children tend to develop trust with others more easily than most adults do. They are usually seeking acceptance, understanding, and somewhere to belong.

The most vulnerable age group for online predators is children between the ages of eleven and fifteen. This is a time when kids are seeking more independence from their parents, testing their limits, exploring their identities, and taking risks. They are essentially more open to new influences, relatively new to the online environment, and are often isolated or lonely and therefore easily lured into the grasp of a predator.

The following story shows how easily tragedy can happen.

There was a thirteen-year-old girl named Jill. She was an average eighth-grade student who liked school and most of her classes—though she was not very good in math.

Jill's best friend was Erin. They were very close, and Jill could confide in Erin about almost anything. Jill lived with her mother, stepfather, and her six-year-old sister, Beth. She was happy at home; she got along with everyone. At times, though, she felt that she didn't have much in common with her parents.

Jill's parents were very busy. Her mother had her own business, and her stepdad traveled a lot for his job. They were a close family but did not spend much time together.

In her free time, Jill played soccer and competed on a girls' team in the city where she lived. When it was not soccer season, she loved to hang out with Erin and her other friends at the mall. She really loved going to the movies and had a secret crush on Ashton Kutcher.

She also loved to surf the Web. There were two computers in her house; one was in her mother's office, which she was not allowed to use, and the other was in the family room. She used the Internet for school assignments and to interact with friends on MSN instant messaging, ICQ, and sometimes in chat rooms. She knew that she should never give out her name and address and to allow only her own group of friends to enter any private chat rooms.

She had found herself surfing the Web a lot more since she broke up with her boyfriend, Todd. Her parents didn't mind, because she was at home and they had just moved the computer into the family room where they could supervise her.

Jill's parents had never been in a chat room or used instant messaging, and they were amazed at how comfortable their daughter was on the computer. Quite often, Jill's mother would find her sitting for hours, late at night, chatting to friends. Jill even signed an Internet contract that listed the safety rules and her responsibilities while she was online, so her mother did not worry about her online safety.

One night, while Jill was chatting with Erin, a new person entered the chat room with a user name of "cute-teen-guy." Jill didn't recognize the handle, but Erin did. She had it in her approved group of chatters. Cute-teen-guy was someone whom Erin had met online and had been talking to for a while. She said he was a nice guy who went to a different high school than theirs. Erin told Jill that he was okay to talk to, so Jill let him into the chat.

Jill and cute-teen-guy had a great chat, and she had so much fun that she didn't want to sign off. They had lots in common, and he was so easy to talk to!

Only after her mother insisted that she go to bed did Jill reluctantly say good-bye. She liked cute-teen-guy, who confided in her that his real name was Bradon.

The next day at school, Jill informed Erin that she liked Bradon and asked if she knew anything else about him. Bradon had told Erin that he went to high school across town and that he was in grade ten. His girl-friend had just broken up with him. Erin had never met him, but thought that he was a friend of a boy in her music class. The connection, although distant and unchecked, was all the encouragement she needed. Jill was happy, and believed that Bradon was who he said.

That night, she logged on and talked for three hours with Bradon. They even went to their own chat room so they could talk in private. They talked about her school and her ex-boyfriend. Bradon confided how much his ex-girlfriend had hurt him; Jill, fresh from a break-up herself, could relate.

She also told Bradon how she loved going to movies, especially Ashton Kutcher movies, and playing soccer. He loved soccer, too, and played on a local team. At this point, Jill was thrilled that Erin had introduced them. She and Bradon talked about friends, movies, and music. He seemed to understand Jill so well!

She was interrupted again by her mother, who asked who she was talking to. "Bradon," Jill replied, "a boy from school." Jill's mom was satisfied with the answer—as long as she wasn't talking to someone she didn't know, her mother thought Jill was safe.

Over the next week, Jill and Bradon talked every night. And on Friday night, Bradon sent Jill his picture. Jill was excited when she opened the file and saw how good-looking he was: he had brown eyes just like Ashton Kutcher!

So when he asked her for a photo, Jill sent Bradon a photo of her and her little sister standing on the lawn in front of their house. She explained that it was not the best picture, since they had just gotten home from the beach when it was taken. Bradon didn't mind, though; he thought Jill was cute and wanted to meet her.

Bradon asked Jill if she wanted to go to a movie with him. She was elated and a bit nervous. What if he didn't like her when they meet? At first she said that she was busy, but Bradon was persistent. After some convincing, he got her to agree to meet at the movies on Saturday at 8 p.m.

Jill immediately called and told Erin all about her upcoming date with Bradon on Saturday night. She was really nervous and asked if Erin wanted to go with her, especially since Jill knew not to meet with anyone alone whom she had met online. Erin agreed to meet her at the box office at 7:30 p.m., before Bradon got there.

Saturday night arrived, and Erin waited outside the box office for Jill. But she never arrived. Erin called Jill's house at 8:30, but her mom said that Jill had told her she was going to meet her friends early, at 6 p.m., as suggested by Bradon.

This story is reflective of a common scenario that illustrates how easy it is for kids to become entwined in a predator's deceit and seduction. Jill made some fatal errors in her online relationship with Bradon. Although she believed that she was safe, she broke several rules that would have kept her secure.

A predator is looking for a way to connect with a child's feelings. He will spend a great deal of time trying to figure out if she is an easy target. Jill discussed her feelings and interests with Bradon, which clearly showed him that she was vulnerable.

Furthermore, when Jill opened the photo attachment that Bradon sent, she could have easily allowed him instant access to her computer and personal information stored on the hard drive. By sending him her photo she offered more information to Bradon, most important what she looked like. Aside from putting herself in further danger, Jill jeopardized her sister and her family by sending a photo that might have assisted him in locating her house. She had already talked about where she went to school, and had given the name of her soccer team and her photo. It would have been easy for Bradon to find her even if she hadn't agreed to meet him at the movies early.

And even though Jill's parents had the intention of keeping her safe online, no one paid close enough attention to the situation to see the warning signs.

Instead of waiting for a predator to choose your child, you will need to be proactive, and keep one step ahead of him. There are warning signs that may lead to your child being a target of an online predator.

Warning Signs from Your Child

- spends all of his time online, even losing sleep to spend more time online
- quickly closes down a screen or shuts the computer off if you walk into the room
- uses Net lingo to prevent you from understanding his conversations
- is vague when confronted about his activities online
- stores pornography on his computer
- uses someone's account, other than his own, to gain Internet access
- receives packages, letters, or gifts in the mail from someone you do not know
- makes long-distance phone calls to numbers you do not recognize

- is withdrawn from other friends or family members, and only wants to be with his online friends

It is illegal for an adult to solicit children for sexual purposes in Canada. This includes luring them over the Internet, sending child pornography, and inviting sexual contact. There are also criminal laws that relate to stalking, harassment, and assault that may apply. In 2001, Child Find (www.childfind.ca) was mandated by the Manitoba Department of Justice to run a cybertip line to safeguard children from Internet crime in Manitoba. Since then, www.cybertip.ca has been created as a secure and non-investigative reporting body to receive tips of online exploitation of children, child pornography, child prostitution, luring, and child-sex tourism. This is the only government-mandated cybertip line in Canada. There are other websites that request you submit tips through them, but www.cybertip.ca should be considered the authority. Cases are reviewed and turned over to local police to investigate further.

To date, the cybertip line is still working hard at raising awareness, educating, and encouraging parents to report all suspicious and inappropriate materials received. Please take advantage of this service: report everything that you feel is suspicious. Do not worry if you are wrong; that is up to the officials to determine. The only thing you need to do, as a parent, is fill out the form and make the report. You can save a child from becoming the next victim—he may even be yours.

Prevention

There are several things that you can do, short of unplugging the computer and Internet for good, to help reduce the risks of predators reaching your kids online. Completely removing the computer does not work. Kids have access to the Internet through their cell phones, video game systems, television, mobile devices, friends, neighbors, schools, Internet cafés, and libraries. Unless you are stranded on a desert island, without a cell phone, you cannot avoid the Internet and the World Wide Web. Nor should you. To help ensure that your kids are safe while online

- learn about the world in which your kids are playing
- establish clear and reasonable guidelines for them
- set sharp and definite punishments for any infractions
- lead by example
- keep the lines of communication open with your kids
- keep the computer in a common area of your house—but do not fall prey to the common belief that no other supervision is needed
- check the history of websites visited on your child's computer by opening your Internet browser and clicking Ctrl+H

You should also teach your children to

- choose a gender-neutral e-mail address that does not have a sexual undertone to it
- never give out their e-mail address unless it is to friends you know
- never give out personal information online
- never open attachments that end in .exe or .zip
- never download files or images without your permission
- never respond to e-mails from people they do not know
- tell you if they have received a message that is disturbing or makes them uncomfortable or scared

Other Risks of the Internet

Although online predators seem to garner the most attention in both media and in the eyes of parents, it is important not to forget that this new environment brings other risks as well.

Cyber-bullying

Bullying in the schoolyard, in the neighborhood, and within a family can cause insurmountable damage to a child's self-esteem, courage, and development. Barbara Coloroso, one of North America's most trusted parenting educators, suggests in her bestselling book *The Bully, the Bullied, and the Bystander* that bullying "is a life-and-death issue that we ignore at our children's peril." Children are being taunted, ridiculed, assaulted, and degraded in massive numbers by their peers every day.

Sadly, not all children withstand the pressure or get the help they need. These are the ones who take their own lives. We seem to hear their stories with alarming regularity, and the link between bullying and the young person's decision to commit suicide is no mere theory: in many cases, the victim leaves a note explaining that bullying has become too oppressive, too hard to manage, and that life has become intolerable. A well-known example of this occurred in November 2000, when fourteen-year-old Dawn-Marie Wesley, from Mission, B.C., hanged herself. Her suicide note named three girls she said were "killing" her because of bullying. Teen suicide resulting from constant aggressive bullying has become such a concern that a new word has been coined to describe it: "bullycide."

Bullying is a difficult problem to address when the attacks are face to face, but even more challenging when the bully is able to get to his or her victims in the comfort and safety of their own homes. With teenagers engaging in so many new forms of digital communication, all of which form a virtual extension of the school environment itself, there are few places left to hide from a persistent cyber-bully.

A cyber-bully is particularly dangerous because he can often communicate his messages with much more anonymity than face-to-face communication, reach his victim easily, and share his hurtful and hateful messages with large numbers of recipients in seconds. And, because the messages are often sent from one child's home to another's, rather than on school property, school administrators have little or no authority.

Instant messaging, chat rooms, text messaging, and cell phones have become tools for cyber-bullies. No longer must they wait to see their targets in person; they can reach them anywhere, at any time. The normal rules of "Netiquette" (which refers to all the unwritten conventions that govern interactions among Internet users) fall by the wayside when cyber-bullies are in control. They may indulge in "flaming," which means sending a deliberately confrontational or derogatory message to others on the Internet. Whatever tactics they use, they make their targets' online experience as unpleasant and humiliating as in the schoolyard, classroom, or lunchroom.

The cyber-bully has an added power over his or her victims. Many victims are afraid of telling their parents for fear that they will overreact and take away their cell phone, computer, or any other technology that gives the cyber-bully access. In this, the kids have a point: although the intention is good, when parents remove all access to these technologies, the one punished is the victim.

Anti-bullying programs and open lines of communication with your child can help reduce her risk of becoming a victim of cyber-bullies, or even becoming a bully herself. Use of the Internet and advanced technology must come with guidelines, rules, and responsibilities. Teach your children to report any threatening or harassing activity to you. Then you must take immediate action. It may be necessary to block the sender's e-mail from coming through, change e-mail addresses and cell phone numbers, or seek help from your school or the local police. Monitor your child's online use instead of removing all access to communication. Complete denial of communication with peers and friends could be as devastating to your child as bullying itself.

Criminal activity

You can find literally anything on the Web. This includes a wealth of "how-to's," from how to build a house, bake a cake, fix your car, or build a pipe bomb. Unless you have filtering software on your computer that has parameters set to prohibit websites with such content, your curious kids can learn how to do anything they choose.

In February 2004, a fifteen-year-old boy from Hamilton, Ontario, met online with another teen from Michigan. The two were first introduced while playing an online weapons game. The trouble came when the boy asked his American friend to mail an AK-47 assault rifle (an illegal weapon in Canada) to his home in Hamilton. In exchange, the Hamilton teen would send two pistols. The American teen sent the parcel through the mail marked as an aluminum baseball bat. Fortunately, the package was checked and stopped at the border.

This case illustrates how easy it is to meet and communicate with others online and even plan criminal activity with them. Your teen can come into contact with people whom he likely would never meet under other circumstances. Teens may engage in collaborative hacking, gambling, transporting of drugs, fraud, and illegal copying of software, music, or other copyrighted material.

To properly combat these crimes, parents need to be diligent in supervising and learning what their kids are doing while online.

Hate messages and propaganda

Hate groups have found new ways to reach unsuspecting targets, including vulnerable, idealistic young teenagers who are looking for a place to fit in. The Internet has allowed hate-motivated groups to join forces, support one another's dangerous and racist beliefs, and encourage others to follow. The number of active hate-related websites worldwide has increased from one in 1995 to an alarming 4,700 in 2004.

Although it is a crime in Canada to incite hatred toward an identifiable group, there is a fine line between freedom of expression and propagating hatred. Hate-motivated websites are damaging, obscene, and invariably represent other groups in false and derogatory ways. Although racial supremacists purport to be proud of who they are, they almost always have a vicious agenda of harassing, expelling, or exterminating another group. If your children have visited a hate-motivated website (you can check their online history by using Ctrl+H) you need to discuss the implications of the disturbing material as soon as possible. (I'll discuss gangs and hate-motivated groups in more detail in chapter seven.)

Internet addiction

An activity can be classified as an addiction if participating in it has negative effects on your life or on the lives of those around you. Internet addiction is a phenomenon that is still being carefully watched by healthcare professionals around the globe. Whether Internet addiction can actually be claimed as a clinical diagnosis is controversial, since many experts and observers believe that using the Internet is more compulsive than addictive.

Regardless of what the medical practitioners agree to disagree on, you as a parent need to understand that overuse and misuse of the Internet can have negative effects on your child's mental and physical health. Not only that, but a child who spends unlimited amounts of time online in chat rooms, message boards, or multi-user games has a higher risk of contact by predators.

As discussed earlier, the Internet is an extremely effective way for a predator to reach your child because he can appear in any guise he chooses. This element of anonymity also attracts youth who are otherwise less socially accepted by their peers. Kids who find it difficult to make friends, are unathletic, awkward, or lonely can find a sense of comfort and belonging in chat rooms. They can present themselves as popular, funny, charismatic people, and attract numerous online friends. These kids will spend hours chatting, socializing, and even "dating" over the Internet, all under a fictitious personality. To a child with a limited social life or peer contact in the outside world, the acceptance he finds on the Net can be seductive, and he can easily get hooked. The irony is that instead of these children becoming confident, and therefore more successful in other relationships, they become more introverted, isolated, and vulnerable.

Aside from making new acquaintances on the Internet, droves of kids, especially teenage boys, are taking part in online multi-user games. This form of entertainment has moved video gaming to a whole new level. Kids can play video games in real time over the Internet, against other players. Most parents were probably hooked themselves, if only for a short time, on Pac-Man or Super Mario. It is difficult to ignore the attraction that these multi-level, multi-player, reality-based games can be to a teen. But some parents report their concern about the many hours their kids spend playing these games, and their concerns are valid.

There are warning signs that your child may be heading toward Internet addiction. If you feel that the following traits describe him, it is time to reassess the entire family's online habits and alter them to support your decision to limit online time.

Some possible symptoms of Internet addiction include

- physical pain, such as headaches, sore eyes, carpal tunnel syndrome, or backache
- loss of sleep
- being obviously happier when online
- slipping grades at school
- loss of interest in friends and family activities
- being drawn to the computer at all times of the day

If you think your child is spending too much time playing online games, chatting, or surfing the Net, you need to intervene quickly. Though it won't be easy, you need to identify what is attracting her to the Net, and help find a healthier substitute. If it is social acceptance, look for outside clubs or organizations she might be interested in joining. If it is gaming, set limits on the time spent on these games. Even though teenagers are busy developing their own identities, your example is still powerful. If they see you spending too much time on your computer, whether working or online, they may feel that you've tacitly given them permission to spend unlimited time in front of their computer as well. Lead by example.

If you feel that your child is beyond discussing the problems of overuse, you may need to seek the help of a professional who deals with addiction. Because Internet addiction is still a relatively new term, you should investigate your options by looking to agencies in your community that deal with addictions more generally. It could be that your child's potential Internet addiction stems from another psychological issue.

Learning the Internet Lingo

Kids who use chat rooms, IM, and text messaging have become accustomed to space and time limitations on their messages. With cell phones, for instance, the space in the screen for messages is very small, which is the reason it is called SMS (for short message system).

To work within the limitations, kids as well as adult chatters often converse in a language called "Net lingo." This is reminiscent of shorthand, with a twist of comedy, personality, and emoticons (which are symbols that convey a feeling or emotion). This new language can be frustrating to a new user and completely confusing to a parent who reads "GTG, POS" on her daughter's cell phone. (By the way, that means, "Got to go, parent over shoulder.")

Net lingo is used not only because of limited space and the need for speed. It is often intentionally cryptic, a code used by kids to keep parents from learning what their Net conversations are about. Unfortunately, predators also learn to speak the lingo, and they can easily identify new users (who may also be younger and less sophisticated) by their lack of terminology. If you want to learn more about this strange language of acronyms, visit www.netlingo.com. BGUTI (better get used to it), because it is not going away.

The Internet has changed the way we work, live, communicate, operate our businesses, pay our bills, bank, and even socialize. It has opened the door to every opportunity, idea, opinion, and belief imaginable. It offers new levels of convenience, knowledge, and power to kids, parents, and families.

But as with any form of media or communication, parents need to insist on responsible use of the Internet and teach their children to question what they hear, read, and view online. Just because the words or images are easily flashed in front of their eyes does not mean that every message is truthful or well-intended. And it is vital to remember that predators can lurk behind the most seemingly innocuous online presence or personality.

The Internet and the World Wide Web do not have to be as confusing as you may think. Of course, there are many aspects of programming and technology that are best left to the techies of the world, but for the most part, parents are capable of successfully navigating the online world. Most important, you need to believe one thing: you can protect your child from predators and other negative influences found on the Net. Safe kids and safe families have taken the time to learn, appreciate, and understand the risks and warning signs involved in this new playground.

Chapter Seven

Danger Has a New Face: Hate Groups Find New Ways to Reach Children

The other night at dinner, my son began to talk about a new boy in his class. He started to describe him not by his personality but by his race. He said this boy was very black and that people who are black "scare" him. I was shocked at what he said and I have no idea where it came from. I am afraid that he will grow up to hate any race that is not Cantonese, like we are.

No human race is superior; no religious faith is inferior. All collective judgments are wrong. Only racists make them.

—Elie Wiesel

It continues to amaze me how cruel we humans can be to one another. As a police officer, I witnessed violent acts that people committed against their so-called loved ones, often because of simple differences of opinion. But when I began to encounter what are called hate-motivated crimes, I saw a level of intimidation, disrespect, and hostility that I had never seen before. Even more alarming to me was how often these ferocious crimes were committed by youths.

There are haters all around us, of all ages, races and genders. They are mothers, fathers, clergy, educators, professionals, politicians, bullies, and yes, even kids. If we were honest with ourselves, we could recall feeling hatred for someone or something in each of our pasts. I can think of times that I truly felt hatred toward a predator who took the innocence of a child. But I hated him not because of where he was from, his race, culture, or gender, but because of his actions.

The definition of hatred is a strong feeling of ill will or dislike. It is a powerful and destructive emotion that can rear its ugly head for many reasons. However, there is a significant difference between realistic and unrealistic hatred.

A contemporary example of hatred took place on September 11, 2001, when a small number of Middle Eastern Muslim extremists hijacked and crashed airplanes into the World Trade Center in New York City and the Pentagon in Washington, D.C., killing thousands of people. That event changed the way the world looks at security, and the way we look at each other.

Many people would say they feel a strong hatred toward the nineteen terrorists. This is realistic hate. However, once people extend this hatred to include all Middle Eastern people or all Muslims, and then act on this hatred, they become no different from the terrorists themselves. They become true haters.

What Is a Hate Crime?

There are many different definitions for what a hate crime is. There are two in the Canadian Criminal Code, as well as a definition in the Canadian Human Rights Act. What you need to know is that a hate crime is committed as a result of the differences (real or perceived) between the offender and his victim. A good definition to keep in mind is that a hate crime is any criminal act committed against an individual or group simply because of their color, race, religion, disability, ethnic origin, sexual orientation, gender, or age.

A hate-motivated crime can affect the surrounding community as well as the main target. For example, if a hater paints a swastika on the side of a synagogue, it is more than just graffiti on the wall of a building: it is a hate crime that will affect many members of the community. Because the hater has used a symbol that represents the largest mass murder in Jewish history, the Jewish population will feel offended, threatened, and perhaps even fearful of its safety. A victim of a hate crime is anyone exposed to the criminal act, or its effects. The number of victims of one hate crime is therefore potentially infinite.

Only about 10 percent of hate-motivated crimes are committed by organized hate groups. The rest are committed by individuals. In Canada, statistics show that hate-related offenses are on the rise, but this is due to the increased intelligence among police agencies and new agreements among police forces about how to recognize and report hate crimes. Still, it is estimated that only one in every fifteen hate-motivated crimes is ever reported to police. Hate-motivated crimes saw a dramatic spike shortly after 9/11, likely due to the increased sensitivity to fear and instability that prevailed at that time. Terrorism instills this kind of fear in its victims, making onlookers more aware, more observant, and more inclined to take a stand, even if that means simply reporting suspected hate crimes to police. Yet the fear subsided, and once again people became desensitized. The reporting of hate-motivated crimes has returned to an average of approximately 400 incidents per year in Canada.

Is Your Child a Hater?

Hatred is a learned emotion. Most child haters develop from uninformed, inattentive parents.

Children are very different from adults in the way they absorb, value, and retain information. Adults have learned not to believe everything they hear. They will often devote more attention to valid information and discard misleading information quickly. Children, on the other hand, absorb good and bad information equally. They will pay as much attention to negative, harmful, misleading information as they will to positive, empowering, and helpful information. Children have not developed a keen and effective "bad information filter" yet, and they often pick up harmful opinions from within their families—even when the family is unaware of expressing a harmful opinion.

The most important source of information for children, especially young children, is their parents or guardians. These individuals will shape a child's impressions of what is right and wrong, good and evil, socially acceptable and criminal. Even a seemingly unimportant matter can make a tremendous difference in a child's outlook toward others and in his actions.

A friend of mine, Christine, is a great parent to her six-year-old son, Jake. She is cautious in what she says about other people around her son. She believes strongly in equality and does not want him to form negative, bigoted opinions of others. She told me an amusing story that illustrates just how powerful our opinions can be in the minds of our kids.

Christine hates only one thing, and that is mushrooms. She hates mushrooms so much that if one even brushes up against another food, she won't eat it. She cannot stand their smell, taste, or texture—in fact, she can barely watch someone else eat them. Everyone knew how much Christine hated all mushrooms, because she made it very clear.

One day, Christine and Jake were at a party celebrating her parents' fortieth wedding anniversary. There was lots of food and fun. A friend of Christine's offered Jake one of her homemade stuffed mushroom caps, displayed beautifully on a tray with melted cheese and parsley for decoration. Jake screamed as if he had witnessed a murder, and vomited directly onto the mushroom caps. Unfortunately, the mushroom maker had a sensitive gag reflex, and she immediately vomited on Jake's head. This caused a wave of kids screaming and running from the horrific sight. Jake cried hysterically because he had vomit in his hair. Christine ran to Jake's side where, unfortunately, the vomit-covered mushrooms on the ground made for a slippery surface. Christine stepped on the slippery mess and fell to the ground, taking Jake with her. As pain shot up her leg, she knew instantly that she had sprained her ankle.

Christine managed to get up and take herself and Jake home without further incident. When they were cleaned up, Christine sat with Jake as she iced her swollen ankle. She asked him why he had vomited, thinking that he must have the stomach flu. Jake replied, "Mushrooms make me sick, Mommy, just like they make you."

Aside from the humorous nature of this unfortunate event, the situation was an eye-opener for Christine. Jake had never eaten mushrooms before, but based on his mother's hatred of the fungi, he strongly believed they were detestable and became physically ill at the sight of them.

That story is about mushrooms, and no one ever really gets hurt from acting on their hatred for mushrooms. But it is not much different from what happens when a child is exposed to racial hatred through his parents' unthinking negative comments, obscene gestures, jokes, and unfair judgments.

Kids soak up their environments and experiences from the time they are born. True haters begin to develop early. As they grow, they begin to form opinions and beliefs based on what they have been told, feel to be true, and experience. Parents who consistently deliver positive, non-biased messages, encourage diversity, and embrace change rarely raise haters.

It is easy for kids to focus on one aspect of a person that their parent may dislike, and quickly apply this dislike to all people who share the same attribute. This could and usually does include racism. True haters can come from all places, races, and socio-economic backgrounds, but are almost always put on an early path to hatred by the significant people in their lives. But parents are not the only ones with influence over a child's belief systems. Even a minor intolerance that reflects a bias from a favorite uncle, cousin, grandparent, or idol can have equal effect.

It is okay for your kids to have a strong dislike for something, or even someone. That alone doesn't make them haters. But if they take action based on the dislike or hatred, they cross the line and become haters. This could take the form of bullying another child, or refusing to help someone in need because of their differences. Hatred is taken to its most destructive extreme when it is generalized into hatred for an entire population, and this is something you have to watch for in your children.

Imagine your child in the following scenarios to see if he or she is on the road to becoming a hater.

Scenario One

Your child, Jim, gets in an argument with another boy, Quan, at school. Quan is Asian and your son is white. Jim is very mad at Quan and tells you later that night that he hates Quan. Although anger can be an alarming and dangerous emotion, Jim's feelings have a basis. He and Quan argued and Jim became angry. You will be able to talk with Jim and help him find the real reason for his anger, and eventually Jim and Quan will again be friends. This is realistic hatred.

Scenario Two

Take the same situation: Jim and Quan get in an argument at school. Jim comes home and tells you that he hates Quan, calls him a derogatory name, and says he hates all Asian people. In the days following, Jim continues to express his dislike for all Asian people, making frequent discriminatory comments about them. This is unrealistic hate—and the beginnings of a true hater.

If the first scenario fits your family dynamic, you are in fine shape. Your child has a reasonable and warranted dislike for an individual, based on his actions. He dislikes only the individual. As children mature, they learn ways to understand and control their anger, and many times kids who feel hatred for each other in grade school become friends in later years. Realistic haters get over it. They do not transfer their anger to all people.

If the second scenario rings bells, you need to take a closer look at your child and the direction he or she is headed. Unrealistic hatred for an identified group of people is one of the most dangerous emotions and beliefs that one can harbor. Adolf Hitler, perhaps the most notorious hater of all, was driven by hate, and he nearly succeeded in exterminating the Jewish people.

History can and often does repeat itself. I saw it every day as a police officer, watching children follow closely in the criminal and violent footsteps of other people. But it doesn't have to. You have the power to make the next generation—your kids—safe, wise, caring, tolerant, and free from hate. In order to achieve this, you need to do two things: be responsible for how your own words and actions will affect your children's attitudes, and watch closely to see if any external influences may cause the seeds of intolerance to germinate and grow in your child. Early intervention can help to prevent the evil of hatred from infiltrating your family.

Hate-Motivated Youth Gangs

In an ideal world, parents would not only exert exclusively positive influences on their children, they would also have control over other influences in their children's lives. But we live in the real world, where parents sometimes make mistakes, and where you may not always know who your kids are being exposed to, or what messages they are receiving.

Up to a certain age, your child is influenced by you more than by anybody else. But by the time he transforms into a new and opinionated self, usually in his early teens, he will be actively seeking outside influences. (I use the word *transforms* because it best describes the personality flip-flop that happened when my son turned thirteen. "Who are you and what have you done with my son?" I wanted to ask this freakish alter ego.)

The older your child grows, the more this rule is true: Your kids are an extension of their friends. To quote a great cliché: "Tell me who your friends are and I'll tell you who you are." You can gain enormous insight into your child's likes, dislikes, beliefs, and future direction by looking at his friends. Sometimes, too, you can read the warning signs, because friends are the most reliable indicators of the kind of person your child is becoming.

If you've managed to keep the lines of communication open with your kids from an early age, your child's transition to adolescence may not even be a concern for you. However, if you did not always have enough time to talk to your kids, were never told that you possessed the power to influence your teen, or if your kids are not willing to share as much as you would like, you need to pick up the slack quickly.

Adolescence is a critical time. A child may feel like an outsider, even within his own family. In the process of becoming his own person he may seek friends who are vastly different from what he has previously known. In his search, he may encounter a hate gang.

Detective Constable Terry Wilson, one of the top hate-crime investigators in Canada, defines a gang as "three or more people that have an identifiable feature or that are involved in anti-social or criminal behavior." A hate-motivated youth gang comes together to encourage, support, and propagate its belief in racial supremacy over others.

There are many extremist movements throughout Canada and the world, but the most common profile of a hate-motivated youth gang are white supremacists. You may have heard them called skinheads or the Ku Klux Klan. These gangs draw national media attention and have been showcased by entertainment talk shows, movies, and other media for years. It is difficult to ignore the screaming white supremacist in the pointy hat ranting nonsense and lies about another race, but unless you witness such severe extremist behavior, you may easily dismiss the possibility that hatred could exist in your own community. It's even harder to believe that kids could be involved.

The fact is that organized hate gangs can be found within any socio-economic group, in any community.

Hate-motivated gangs usually characterize themselves, at least initially, as having "pride" in their own race. They do not initially say others are less valuable than themselves, but rather build on the sense of pride for who they are. This is the shield they hide behind. There is a clear value in taking pride in oneself and one's heritage; however, as soon as this pride is reflected and expressed by beating down another group for its differences, it becomes hatred.

The haters look for kids who are in a transition in their lives and are looking for a sense of belonging. Perhaps they are students who have just entered high school and suddenly find themselves dropped from the top rung of the social ladder (eighth grade in public school) to the bottom (ninth grade in high school). Some of these kids will focus entirely on finding a place and group to fit into—which the hate-motivated gang is only too happy to provide.

Hate-gang involvement: warning signs

Each warning sign on its own can mean little, but if you find that several describe your child and situation, you will need to take action.

1. Sudden change of friends. Your child is looking for a sense of family. This is what makes him a prime target. If he is approached by a group that can give him what he feels he is missing, he will suddenly and drastically exclude any other friends or family that he used to spend time with.

2. Obsessing over something new. A child who is involved in a hate gang will begin to obsess over things that he may not have otherwise cared about. It may be a particular fashion or something political. His behavior will change sharply and radically.

3. Change of dress. Almost all gangs have possessions that are prized for their symbolic value. For some, it is a particular color, or a specific item of clothing. For white supremacist gangs, it is often black bomber jackets, high black leather military boots with white shoelaces, and green suspenders worn down. The boys will have shaved heads and the girls will have mostly shaved heads but leave the bangs and sides long. They will have tattoos of swastikas, an "SS" in the shape of two lightning bolts, or other symbols of hatred.

It can be difficult to distinguish between legitimate fashion trends and hate-gang dress. A reliable way to know is by looking at other kids in the community. Are they all wearing the same clothing or hairstyles? If it is common to the average youth, it is likely just fashion and will change next year. However, if you notice that it is unique to your son and his friends, you should consider this a warning sign. If you are not sure, ask them why they dress the way they do. If they say, "It shows pride in my race," you have a problem that you need to address immediately.

4. Hate graffiti. Hate-gang doodlers may draw swastikas, negative and violent depictions of people of another race, derogatory slang, or any symbol that depicts their hatred for an identifiable group. These doodles often begin either on their school books or on the inside pages. They do this to see if anyone else in their class is like-minded. This person will often be new to the hate movement, and will use doodling to test the waters and the reactions of those around him. You must address any suspicious doodles and symbols on your child's belongings. If you do not intervene at this early stage, your silence will be taken as approval, and your child will become more confident in his beliefs.

The next stage of doodling is public displays of hate graffiti where everyone can view these negative expressions—such as on a bus shelter or mail boxes. Finally, the hater will move to specific targets for his hate messages, such as mosques, synagogues, or other meaningful property of his identified targets. Hate graffiti is not art; it is a cowardly, repugnant display of intolerance.

5. Sudden interest in politics. Kids who become involved in a hate-motivated gang will suddenly have a propensity for politics. They will watch the news, read the papers, and have clear opinions on world events. The more entrenched they are, the more vocal they will be. There is a difference between your teen demonstrating that he is simply growing up, with a mind and opinions of his own, and making comments that are questionable such as, "They should stop letting in the immigrants," or using derogatory slang about another ethnic group. The reason teens tend to vocalize their opinions is that they are testing to see if they will get support from home with their belief.

If you see your child in the descriptions above, there is still something you can do for her. If you believe your child is involved in a hate-motivated group, you may need to seek outside help. Removing your child from a hate-motivated gang is very similar to making a cult intervention. Remember that in order for the hate gang to get your child to accept its views, politics, and values, it has spent a great deal of time encouraging her, supporting her, and assuaging the loneliness she felt when she came into contact in the first place. By now, your child will feel a sense of belonging, family, and loyalty that will be hard to break. Confront your child with your suspicions only if you feel that you will garner a positive outcome where you can further discuss your concerns. Do not confront her simply out of anger.

What to do if your child is involved in a hate-motivated group

Who do you turn to for help? It's unlikely that friends or family members will be effective in persuading your child to leave the group, since he has probably alienated all former influences from his life and has totally isolated himself, except from the other gang members. You will need to look outward for help to social workers, counselors who specialize in gang psychology, or even the police if you fear for your child's safety. Many parents do not want to involve the police, and that is understandable. However, there are avenues through many police departments, such as Family and Victim Services, which may assist in a referral to an expert for help.

If your child is a hard-core hater, you will need to clearly explain to him that you will not support his racist choices. This may mean that your child will have to move out of your home. It may mean that he or she will become entrenched, for a time at least, in the hate movement. You may feel a complete sense of loss and frustration at not being able to influence his decisions and change his attitudes. Do not lose sight of the fact that your child has been convinced he is doing the right thing and has a new "family" that understands him.

You must continue to make it very clear that you cannot support his actions or beliefs while he is still in the movement. You should explain that if he ever wanted to leave the movement and come home, he would be welcome. You will be there for him, regardless of what he has done or what he believed to be true while in the movement. But while he is still a hater, you cannot accept him.

This is a very difficult stand to take as a parent, but it is vital that you show your child your conviction in your own beliefs. If he believes, even for a moment, that he may convince you he is right in his hate system, it will be even more difficult to get him out of the movement.

What makes it difficult for a youth to leave a gang is that becoming a member has necessitated that she isolate herself from friends, family, and all other contacts that might turn her from the gang influences. A member of a hate-motivated gang believes that she should not trust anyone other than the gang members themselves.

Anyone who is persuaded, by whatever means, to leave a gang, is in for a period of terrible loneliness. A young person leaving a hate gang, or any gang culture, will need support from his family to get him through the painful feelings of separation, displacement, and isolation he will inevitably feel. You need to encourage him that he will again make friends, have relationships, and become part of his community. Your success will depend on your commitment to his safety. Take advantage of all resources within your community, and support him in his loneliness. If he continues to feel isolated, the chances of his returning to the gang for support will greatly increase.

Preventing your child from becoming a hater
As with any potential danger facing your children, there are warning signs that will assist you in identifying and responding appropriately to the threat of gang violence and hate-motivated groups. You can prevent your child from being lured into the arms of a hate-motivated gang.

1. Intervene at an early stage. As a parent you must intervene from the first time you notice a change or comment that may be questionable.

If your child at age nine says he hates all Chinese people, you must not let the comment pass without remark. If a racist belief is planted in his mind, every future comment or observation that he hears will make the belief grow.

What should you say? Let's take a look at Scenario Two again. Jim gets into an argument with Quan at school and decides, based on this situation, that he hates all Asian people. In response, you must find the time to identify other Asian people within your community, on TV, in cartoons—anything that can help you show Jim, in concrete ways, that he does not hate all Asian people. Convey to him that all people, regardless of their differences, deserve equal respect. Jim will soon find it difficult to continue with his argument and you will be able to address what is really bothering him about his encounter with Quan. Keeping the lines of communication open is a powerful tool.

2. Resist making generalizations. You can be adding to your child's hatred by making sweeping statements about another people. When you say things such as "Chinese people can't drive" or "All used car salesmen are thieves," it is very confusing to an impressionable child. He is looking to you, his parent, to guide him. Even though your comments may only be in jest, they have the potential to sway him toward forming a prejudice with no basis.

3. Be consistent, not conflicting. Teach your child by example. This is the fundamental criterion in raising safe kids. They need your guidance and, most of all, need to trust that you believe your own words. If you preach one lesson, and they see you doing the opposite, they will look for a more trustworthy source. You need to be their source.

4. Get to really know your kids. Invest as much time as you can in really getting to know your kids. Not just what their favorite toys, colors, and cartoons are, but what they are all about. They are little adults in waiting, impressionable, needy, and, most of all, willing to share. Taking an interest in your child accomplishes two vital things. First, it tells her how much you care about her, making it less likely she'll need to look elsewhere for belonging. Second, if you really know your child, you will notice right away if something is different. It could be a comment or gesture that is unlike her, a sudden change in dress, friends, or behavior. If you know your kids well, you will be able to intervene as soon as the first warning sign appears.

How to know if your child is a target of a hate crime

I am often asked why some people become targets. What makes some the unlucky ones? Can we blame society, race, religion, fate, or simply dumb luck?

Some people will always be targets, simply because of their commitment to a specific lifestyle, religion, or belief. Children are raised within the guidelines and belief systems their parents pass on to them and therefore they too may become targets for an opposing group. There is nothing wrong with being a target. In fact, having a solid family belief system and commitment to values is very powerful and will only make your kids and family stronger. It is acceptable to be a target, as long as you recognize that you are.

There are two sides to every crime: the target and the offender. I prefer to use the term "target" rather than victim. A victim will always have once been a target, but a target will not always be a victim. If you find that your children are potential targets, you have the ability, through choices and actions, to ensure that they do not become victims and, most important, not victims for life.

Finding out that your child is being targeted by a group or an individual motivated by hate is frightening, alarming, and sometimes a bit of a blow to your ego. After all, you think your child is not only perfectly normal, you think he's fantastic, so why would others see him as a target?

To find out, all you need to do is ask. If your child comes home and tells you that he is being bullied, harassed, or intimidated by someone else, instead of asking him what he did to cause the harassment, ask him, "Why do you think that person is picking on

you?" Don't settle for the standard "I don't know"; use some forensic interviewing techniques to give you a hand. (I'll discuss these
techniques in detail in chapter nine.) For instance, try asking the
question this way: "If someone else was getting picked on, other
than you, what do you think the reason would be?" Your child will
feel safer answering this question truthfully. He may say, "Because
he acts like a girl," or "Because he has brown skin," or some other
insightful answer. It may be that your child is timid, shy, effemi-
nate, dresses differently from other kids, is poor at sports, has a
learning difference, or there is some other reason that makes him
unlike the group.

What will keep your child from becoming a repeat victim will be
his ability to report the incident the first time. Gangs and bullies
choose targets they will be able to victimize easily, targets who are
weak, fearful, and unsupported by authorities. A hate-motivated
bully will choose a target based on his biases, and then take small,
safe steps to test how easy it will be to turn him from a target to a
victim. If he fails early, is reported, and receives consequences for
his actions, he will move on.

Your child needs to be able to report to you that someone made a
racial or biased comment or action toward him. Then you must
take swift and immediate action. Even if it is a passing racial slur
directed toward your child at school, you need to advise the principal immediately and he or she must confront the offender. Encourage your child to be proud of who he is, regardless of his
differences. Keep the lines of communication open and he will tell
you while it is still early enough to do something about it.

If Your Child Is a Victim

1. Take rational steps to stop it. Revenge and retaliation may at first
seem like your best option. It is painful and even sickening to see
your child hurt, especially when hate is the motivator. However, as
a parent, you have to recognize that your child likely had to drum
up a lot of courage to tell you about this in the first place, and may

be fearful of retaliation for telling. You must teach her how to effectively and rationally react to hate-motivated abuse.

Set up a meeting with the school principal to discuss your concerns. If you fear for your family and child's safety, or you feel that a criminal offense has occurred, consider calling the police. If it is a hate crime, the laws have recently grown some sharp teeth to help combat this dangerous and unacceptable criminal motivation. Prove to your kids that you are not afraid.

2. Resist the temptation to fight back with more hate. Lead by example. Although "an eye for an eye" feels right initially, in the long run it simply perpetuates the problem. Hatred exists on a spiral that needs to be broken. Show your child that you will not give in to feelings of hatred.

3. Silence is deadly: speak up. Telling your child to walk the other way and ignore the hate-motivated bully is the wrong response. He needs to know that when he tells you, you will respond rationally and swiftly. Hatred and racism need to be confronted. Inaction by a victim or his parents essentially condones hatred. Silence does not solve the problem. Hatred is killed by facing it and by clearly telling the haters that you will not tolerate it—period.

The Internet and Hate

The fastest-growing community of hate mongers can be found on the Internet. From one hate site in 1995, the total grew to approximately 4,700 in 2003. These sites promote hatred through message boards, writings, music, and products. They will often call themselves "pro-white" or "pro-black" or "pro" something. But don't be fooled—they are haters and against everyone else. If your child is looking at these sites, and you don't know about them, filter them, or prevent your child from viewing them, you are condoning their hate messages by your silence.

In the 1980s and early '90s there were organized hate groups in cities and communities across Canada. They would commit visible and disturbing acts of hatred in their own territory, and would sometimes get together for rallies or organized functions to meet other haters elsewhere, but they acted more or less independently of one another.

Now, with the Internet, individual acts of violence are supported by a worldwide web of haters. A single hater in a remote area, with the help of the Internet, suddenly has a family of supporters. Don't just look for sexual predators on the Net, keep sharp eyes for the haters because they are out there in force.

Are Youth Gangs the Same as Hate-Motivated Gangs?

Yes. They are similar in the sense that they are gangs, and are all involved in anti-social or criminal behavior. The youth gang culture is present in all cities and most communities in Canada. It is not just an American problem but a serious risk quite possibly in your own backyard.

Gang vs. Group

You see a group of youths hanging around the mall parking lot, smoking and leaning against cars. Is it a gang, or just a group of kids who might—or might not—cause some trouble? There is a distinct difference between a gang and a friendship group.

A gang is a group of three or more people who share an identifiable feature and are involved in criminal or anti-social behavior. A gang uses some physical marker (usually an item of clothing or a symbol on their clothing) to let others know they are part of a gang and to identify other members easily. If you have a group of five kids who are harassing others, stealing cars, or committing crimes, but they do not have an identifiable feature, they are not technically an organized gang.

A friendship group has a lot of movement in and out of the group. Kids will easily come and go from time to time. There may be three or four close friends who form the core of the group, but a new friend or girlfriend may be brought in, then later leave. A friendship group can commit crime and behave anti-socially, but there is an ebb and flow of people coming and going. Their motivation is friendship and peer acceptance. Friendship groups are obvious in schools because of their physical positioning. A friendship group will stand in a circle facing each other. They are focused on the group, on each other, and not interested in outside influences.

A gang does not work that way. They are a solid group with rituals, initiations, and rules. It can be difficult to get into a gang, and difficult to leave. Gangs are motivated by common goals, which may be drugs, money, or simply power. The physical positioning of a gang is much different from a friendship group. Gang members will stand with their backs together, looking out. They are looking for potential targets or threats, and protecting their group.

An established youth gang is not always searching for recruits; in fact, it is usually the other way around. The gang provides the social environment and sense of belonging that the recruit is looking for. To protect your children, you need to look at them from within: are they searching for belonging? Do they feel they are missing something in their lives? Invest time in your kids to identify these needs and try to fill them before outside influences—the kind that are negative and potentially deadly—step in to take up the slack.

What Kids Believe about Gangs
1. Gangs offer a sense of family. The myth is that the gang will remain a family through thick or thin. Kids are looking for unconditional love and acceptance, and are duped into believing that a gang will give them this. But gang members often turn against each other, which is a hard and sometimes violent lesson that many kids learn. A gang is a conditional family and members are assessed and accepted based on what they can bring to the gang.

2. Being in a gang brings prestige and power. Gang members appear to have power, money, girls, drugs, and the freedom to live as they choose. This is a myth that gangs cultivate through music, videos, and dress. But the gang's limited power comes from preying on other people's fears, and the prestige is only perceived within the gang itself. The larger outside world sees gang members as among the lowest people in society and equates power and prestige with being educated, talented, and successful, not with being a street criminal. There comes a time that many gang members realize that gang power and prestige are mirages, and have no substance.

3. Gangs provide protection. One of the greatest myths professed by gangs is that they will provide protection to their members. The truth is that, especially in gang-infested areas, a child who joins a gang has succeeded only in multiplying his enemies (sometimes by the hundreds) simply by association. Becoming part of a gang elevates your risk of harm and potentially death. Being in a gang does not provide protection; it is actually one of the most dangerous places to be.

Are Gangs in Your Child's School?

Gang members are very good at going to school. They are not very good at going to class, but they will be at school, as long as the principal allows them to be. School is the social center for kids between the ages of twelve and eighteen.

Parents need to have good communication with their children's school. Don't be afraid to ask if there is any gang activity in the school and, if so, what the school is doing about it. Communication among parents, schools, and police needs to be continuous and seamless. If parents believe their child is a target or victim of a gang, they need to speak to school officials immediately. Many schools have policy in place to deal with such problems; however, it is up to the parents to bring the issue to the school. The school has the same responsibility. Like hate-motivated crime, gang activity is fed by silence. In order to protect your child and school from gangs, you, the school, or the police will need to intervene early.

Schools are, in essence, communities unto themselves. Some of the people within the community may be predators, haters, gang members—or they may be leaders, innovators, and activists. There are social norms, rules, procedures, and plans—but also disorder, fear, loss, and even tragedy. Too often, parents do not look as closely as they should at their schools. Children of all ages, with open minds and hearts, are turned over to the waiting arms of school 180 days a year, for thirteen years. You need to know that what your children are experiencing, both in class and on the playground, is not only positive but safe.

Chapter Eight

School Safety: How Does Your School Measure Up?

When I leave my child at school I assume that she will be safe. But then I hear about the increase in school violence, shootings, and strangers wandering the hallways. How can I be sure that my child's school really is safe?

In a 1999 poll conducted by CNN, more than half the parents in the United States feared for their child's safety at school. In Canada, parents, educators, and even kids have worried about their safety while at school. Although high-profile school shootings seem to garner most of the attention, children are more at risk of bullying, fights, gang violence, and substance abuse than of being murdered while at school. But the worries I've just named aren't inconsequential. Ensuring that your child will be safe at school is an important and difficult task, and a crucial part of keeping your kids safe.

From kindergarten through high school, kids face a variety of risks that will test their readiness, as well as yours. Part of growing up safely is recognizing situations that may be dangerous and knowing how to respond to them. Most parents are diligent in child-proofing their homes when their babies become mobile, often spending time and money on cabinet locks, window guards, and electric socket covers. Most people also realize there is nothing better than supervision and use these child safety products only as an added layer of protection.

What is of concern is how often this supervision and attention to detail falls short when children are turned over to the schools. The problem is that most parents assume our schools are inherently safe. After all, schools are overseen by governments, who ensure that the necessary policies and procedures are in place. And those who run the schools day-to-day are committed to keeping kids safe. If there was a problem, surely the politicians and the administrators would do something about it, right?

What's the Worst That Could Happen?

Thousands of children walk through school doors each morning in Canada and thousands of kids return home happy, healthy, and unharmed. But that is not always the case.

- In 1997, Ontario public schools reported that 28,000 children were hurt in public playgrounds.
- In 1998, ten-year-old Myles Neuts was found hanging by his shirt on a washroom coat hook at a school in Chatham, Ontario. He later died.
- In 1998, nine students at a Windsor, Ontario, high school were subjected to a strip search by their vice-principal and gym teacher, after a student complained that $90 had been stolen from him.
- In 1999, a grade nine student embarked on a shooting rampage at his school in Taber, Alberta, killing one student and injuring another.
- In 1999, it was estimated that one out of thirteen students in the U.S. had made a suicide attempt that year.
- In 2001, a fourteen-year-old boy was suspended after ripping a pair of tear-away pants off a female student, leaving her standing in her underwear.
- In 2002, a fourteen-year-old student in Halifax, Nova Scotia, shot himself in his bedroom because he was being bullied by classmates.
- In 2002, a man followed a thirteen-year-old girl into school and attempted to hide in the washroom.

- In 2003, seven Alberta teens were killed by an avalanche while on a school-organized ski trip near Rogers Pass, B.C.
- In 2004, in Thunder Bay, Ontario, four-year-old Allyceea Ennis was accidentally killed while riding a school bus en route to daycare. There was no adult supervision on the bus other than the driver.
- In 2004, a former teacher at an elite private school in Toronto, Ontario, was found guilty of nine counts of indecent acts against former students.

These are only a small sample of school-related tragedies that have occurred in Canada over the past several years. They are not typical, but tragedies at school do happen, as these stories show. Although millions of dollars and sincere commitment by professionals are constantly invested into making sure that schools are safe, the bottom line is that the school itself does not determine safety, it is the situations and the people within them that make the difference.

Think Situations, Not Places

When you think about safety, think of it in terms of situations, not places. A school is a place, a building like any other. Just because your children are at school does not mean that they will be safe, unless the teachers, administrators, parents, and student body commit to making every situation as safe as possible.

Parents too often do not inspect their children's schools closely enough. Many simply don't know what questions to ask, or have the boldness to ask them. In my generation, we were told that principals and teachers were the authority to be listened to, not questioned. This rule was so entrenched that some parents today still find it difficult to stand up to principals and teachers, even when it comes to the safety and future of their kids.

The following is a story of my own that demonstrates how far school safety has come in less than thirty years.

I grew up and attended public school in a small town on the outskirts of Vancouver, British Columbia. I spent my grade school years as well as high school in the same town, with the same kids. Back then, we never locked our doors, did not have call display, and were acquainted with almost everyone in the community.

The principal of my grade school lived in the same town, as did most of the teachers. For the most part our town was free of crime, or so we liked to think.

One day, when I was in grade five, I was playing outside the school yard during my lunch hour. It was a day like any other, until a few minutes before the lunch bell rang to end the break, when the principal came out to the playground and told me my mother had called to ask that I go home. He didn't know why because the message was taken by a student assistant who had been answering the office phones during the lunch hour.

I didn't think too much of it other than being pleased that I didn't have to stay for the rest of the day. Free day, I thought. I collected my books and left school for home. We lived only about a ten-minute walk from school, a route that normally took me from the front doors of the school, around the corner to where I dropped off my friend, then up a main street to my home.

This day, however, was different. It was a beautiful day, so I decided to take the back route, through the sports field, across the track, and up the street that backs onto ours. I cut through our neighbor's, hopped the fence, and walked through the unlocked back door to my house.

When I walked in, I could not hear my mother. I didn't see her purse, which she always left on the kitchen counter, and the car was not home. But, being a kid, I didn't think much about it. I made a snack, watched TV, and waited for my mom.

She came home shortly after and was surprised to see me with a bowl full of potato chips, watching TV when I was supposed to be at school. I told her the school principal said that she had called and told me to come home.

The color ran from my mother's face. I had never seen her so white.

She didn't say a word, just walked to the phone and immediately called the school.

After a few minutes, I learned that she had never called the school. The police were called, and an investigation begun. It was later learned that there was a suspicious car parked outside of the school around the time that I was told to go home. There was no call display in those days, so the police could not trace the caller. The student who took the call was certain it was a female caller who said she was my mother and that I was to go home.

My father was a well-known and successful businessman. He believed, as did the police, that someone had made the call in an attempt to set up a kidnapping. For some reason, I chose to walk a different route home. The change of routine may have saved my life.

At that time, my school did not have a safety plan. There was no policy set to deal with such phone requests, no follow-up, no safe schools committee. Nothing.

I know that, today, this scenario is unlikely to happen. Schools should, and often do, have better methods of tracking phone calls, and a policy that would prevent anyone from telling an eight-year-old girl to walk home alone, in the middle of the day, because of an unverified phone call. To be sure, ask your principal how he or she would deal with such situations.

Yet, if schools are safer now, why are the following statements still true?

- I could walk into almost any school, wander the halls, and leave without anyone asking a single question.
- I could call almost any school and ask for the names and phone numbers of students who wish to babysit. I would receive a list without being questioned.
- Parents continue to receive notices from schools telling them to clearly write their children's names in their belongings.
- Kids know who the bullies are, but the teachers don't.

- Kids continue to get seriously injured or even killed while at school, they get lost or hurt on school trips, lured away from school yards, use drugs, cigarettes and alcohol, or sustain sexual, physical, or mental abuse while attending school.

These things can and do still occur even though there is abundant talk and time spent on addressing safe school policies. But talk is cheap and it seems to take a whole lot of time to make some common-sense decisions.

A school is essentially a community with its own social norms, leaders, politics, and even crime. There are rules set out by the leader, the principal, that all must follow. There are guidelines that address everything from proper dress, to curriculum standards and even appropriate games and lessons.

Public schools in Canada, for the most part, reflect a diverse cross-section of cultures, religions, beliefs, languages, and sexual orientations. Because of the diversity, schools find themselves with needs that are as unique as the students within them. However, schools are often burdened with financial cutbacks, small and often ineffective parent councils, and larger class sizes. It is not easy to run schools these days, and even more difficult to keep them safe. As a parent, you need to understand the real hazards facing your kids while they are at school and pay close attention to how your school is addressing each.

Violence in Schools

Contrary to what some people think, violence in school is not increasing. Actually, according to recent studies, it is relatively unchanged. A small number of youth commit the majority of violent crimes. It is difficult to determine the true extent of youth violence in Canada, mainly because the definition and reporting of youth crime varies among investigative bodies. There are also likely many violent incidents involving youth that are never reported to the police and therefore never accounted for in the statistics.

There are three forms of youth violence according to Health Canada: emotional, physical, and sexual abuse. Emotional abuse is often the starting point for bullying in schools. This can include insults, humiliation, threats, destroying property, stalking, or any other degrading behavior that limits the victim's freedom. Physical abuse involves anything physical, including punching, grabbing, pushing, slapping, or use of a weapon causing physical harm. Sexual abuse is any unwanted sexual contact through either threats of physical force or actual physical assault.

A recent survey conducted by the Canada Safe Schools Network reported the following.

Among elementary school students,
  18 percent have been threatened
  13 percent have been physically assaulted
  23 percent report being afraid of other students

Among high school students,
  15 percent have been threatened
  13 percent have been physically assaulted
  19 percent report being afraid of other students

This report shows that elementary school children are being victimized slightly more often and are more fearful than older kids. Almost one-quarter of students are afraid of another child in their school. This is worrisome, because in order for kids to learn, they need to feel safe.

As a parent, find out if your child is fearful of others. If she identifies another student, open the conversation to try to get to the root of the problem. Your child may be in a temporary disagreement with another child, or it may be serious and involve threats or even assault.

Discuss your concerns with the principal and ask specific questions that deal with violence in schools. Do not ask questions about policy, since you will only get vague, even noncommittal answers. Policy is meant to cover all the bases, and to make sure that every school is following the same methods in dealing with problems; policy, however, is just a set of words on a page. You need to know who the principal is as a leader, supporter, and educator. You need to know that he or she will be raising your child with the same integrity as you. Ask questions that will elicit personal responses, not formalized, politically safe ones.

In my experience, principals welcome parents' initiatives and concerns, and are more than willing to discuss their position on each matter. Principals seek the best for your kids, and they will usually do anything it takes to ensure that they are well cared for, safe, and secure while in their care.

Here are some valid questions that you should be asking of your school principal in relation to school violence.

- Are the administration and teachers notified when a child with a violent past is enrolled at the school?
- How do you handle incidents of violence at school?
- How do you deal with incidents of bullying?
- What kind of programs does the school have in place to teach anti-bullying and anti-violence?
- If my child is involved in a violent incident at school, how quickly will you notify me?
- How do you deal with negative, racially motivated comments?
- Does the school strictly enforce zero tolerance for breaches of safety issues such as bullying, violence, weapons, and drugs?
- Has there ever been an incident involving a student bringing a weapon to school?

All of these questions deserve clear, specific answers. If you do not receive answers that satisfy you, do not give up. Continue to ask them until you get the answers you need. If you don't like what you hear, you may need to take your concerns directly to the school board superintendent. The rule is, don't stop until you are satisfied that your child will be safe while in the school's care.

Zero tolerance does not equal zero victims

Schools today have policies in place to deal with an array of safety issues, some of which are bullying, abuse, crime, property damage, and violence. Many school boards now use the term *zero tolerance* to deal with any infractions against school rules; in fact, those words are written into some school board policy. What this means is that no investigation or judgment is required from the school principal; automatic, swift, harsh, and consistent punishment follows without question. If a child breaks almost any school rule, or the law, they face immediate suspension or expulsion from school.

There have been many cases to show that zero tolerance both works and doesn't. Because zero tolerance was adapted from an American model, some of the most bizarre and memorable cases have originated there. In 1999, a six-year-old boy in Colorado Springs was suspended under a zero tolerance drug policy when he gave another child a lemon drop candy. The teacher did not recognize the candy package and called the ambulance. Once it was discovered that the small, pill-like candy was indeed a sweet, the school still upheld the half-day suspension because they had a zero-tolerance drug policy.

This may seem extreme, but such stories abound. In 2002, an eleven-year-old boy in New York died of complications due to asthma because the school's zero tolerance policy prevented him from carrying an inhaler to school. In the same year, thirty-three kindergarten children were suspended due to mandates of zero tolerance. Their transgressions ranged from using their fingers as guns while playing in the schoolyard, to consuming vitamins on school property. In Canada, a twelve-year-old Halifax girl was suspended for pushing another girl, her friend, into a snowbank.

These ridiculous cases aside, the argument for zero tolerance is, of course, that it acts as a general deterrent. If kids know there will be instant punishment for breaking any rules, the thinking goes, they won't break the rules. If that really worked, there would never be a child grounded by a parent! Studies show that even the worst deterrent possible, the death penalty, doesn't stop someone who is determined to murder. So how can we expect that children will choose not to break the rules because suspension will result?

The fact is that zero tolerance does not prevent victims. It is a reactive measure at best, since zero tolerance only comes into play once a victim has been made. Policy that only *reacts* makes way for victimization. It is simply too little, too late. Besides, interpreting zero tolerance policy can be confusing to many who are called upon to use it. Is it zero tolerance toward the actual behavior or toward the individual students?

Zero tolerance as a means to end violence in schools is inadequate and ineffective for several reasons.

1. It cannot address the majority of violence, since most happens off school property (although the initial target is found during school).
2. It is unfair. Each situation is different, and victims who defend themselves are often suspended along with the offenders.
3. It takes all the thinking away from the front line—teachers and principals—and closes any doors to problem-solving opportunities.

Having clear, fair, proactive policies in place that encourage a cooperative approach to violence is far more effective than zero tolerance. Thankfully, although zero tolerance is written into many school policies, often the principal herself takes the time to learn about each incident and uses common sense, sound judgment, and problem solving before resorting to zero tolerance.

As a parent, do you know if your school follows zero tolerance policy? If you are not sure, take five minutes the next day you take your child to school and ask the principal. You need to know where your principal stands on this very important and often controversial procedure.

Sexual Harassment and Abuse

There are two types of sexual offenders your child may face: an adult predator who is a child molester, or another child who is a sexual offender. Both are found in school settings and they are equally dangerous.

A school is a building full of children taught to listen and respect their teachers and coaches, and to obey the rules of the school. They are more or less "ruled" by others in authority. A predator, specifically a pedophile, will seldom work in an isolated profession. He is much more likely to seek employment where children are abundant, including teaching and educational services.

School boards have come to recognize the attraction that a school environment holds for pedophiles. Most have initiated policies whereby all employees must submit a clear criminal records check and (in certain provinces) a child welfare check prior to employment. This is meant to be a deterrent to those who have sex offense records. However, each province, and the various school boards within them, have initiated these rulings quite recently, in some cases fewer than ten years ago. Usually, these rulings state that all *new* employees must submit a clear check, but they do not pertain to all employees already working within the educational system. If you were already employed as a teacher, coach, or custodian before the statute passed, you are exempt from the requirement. For obvious reasons, these rulings have flaws.

Pedophiles have an average of thirty victims before the first report comes to police. Many criminal charges of sexual assault are pled down in court to the lesser offense of assault. Simple assault can mean a push or a slap—hardly the same degree of seriousness as the sexual assault of a child. However, an assault conviction will likely impact a prospective teacher or custodian applicant, while a sexual assault disguised as simple assault can be easily explained away as something far less significant.

By having all school employees submit to a criminal records check, schools are beginning to give themselves a layer of protection from predators. The method is far from perfect, but it is a start.

I feel certain it has deterred some dangerous people from even attempting to be part of a school environment.

Though we continue to hear about cases involving sexual abuse of children by school staff, these incidents are decreasing. Credit for that should go to school boards that insist on stricter screening of all employees, and higher levels of education and training for supervisors, who can now recognize at-risk kids and staff. Anti-abuse programs in schools are helping too. And kids are getting smarter and braver.

Child-on-child sexual abuse is a topic that is not often discussed, but it is a serious risk facing children at school. There is no age limit when it comes to sexual offenders. There are sexual offenders who have victimized classmates through sexual harassment and assault. Children who become sexual offenders are likely to be victims themselves of regular abuse. Proper training of school faculty in identifying possible victims of abuse is essential in helping to prevent sexual violence from perpetuating itself among students. Awareness, open communication, and anti-abuse education for students is crucial. Students should be encouraged to report any sexual incidents that make them uncomfortable or frightened.

School principals must be prepared to ensure the safety of all children in their care, including the offender. Here are some questions you need answered in relation to sexual abuse.

- Does the school inform parents immediately of any safety concerns involving teacher-student conduct?
- What would the school do if they learned of misconduct by a staff member?
- Does the school's screening policy apply to all people who come in contact with your child while at school? Does this include administrators, volunteers, custodians, security, bus drivers?

Unwanted Visitors

Here's a test you can do yourself: attend your child's school during class time and walk through the hallways. Carry a lunch bag if you like (props are a favorite trick used by successful predators). Walk through the school for as long as it takes before someone challenges who you are and why you are in the school. You will likely be surprised at how long it takes, if indeed it happens at all.

School doors are left unlocked during school hours in case a fire or other emergency situation requires immediate evacuation. Although this practice keeps kids from being locked inside, it also allows intruders inside.

There are ample cases in schools across Canada where intruders have been found wandering the hallways, or hiding in washrooms, corridors, or other areas of the school. These intruders have either followed a student into the school or walked in on their own. In fact, in some schools, fear is so high that parent volunteers take shifts standing guard at each door to ensure that no intruders enter during the school day without authorization.

The fear of intruders in schools has also called governments to action. In 2004, the Ontario provincial government agreed to consider funding the installation of video surveillance in elementary schools across Ontario. This came after a rash of sexual assaults took place when intruders entered schools unnoticed. Of course, video surveillance is effective if it is monitored constantly but falls short if one believes that he or she is instantly protected by these new sets of eyes. Surveillance is often the only witness to a crime.

The best way to deal with unwanted visitors is to encourage all staff to challenge anyone they do not recognize, every single time. Washrooms should be checked regularly, all classrooms not being used should be locked, and any suspicious behavior should be reported immediately to the police.

Children should always use the buddy system when going to and from the washroom or even bringing notes to the office. Very young children, up to grade three, should not travel the hallways of the school without teacher supervision during class time. The buddy system does not work for a pair of five-year-olds, since neither is capable of making safe choices when confronted by an adult. Protecting each other would likewise be impossible.

You can't lock all of the doors to a school, but you can keep the lines of communication open. Teachers and administrators should remind parents not to wander the hallways themselves. If they need to visit a classroom, insist that they sign in at the front office and wear a visitor's name tag. If a parent is resistant to following the school's rules, they may give in if they are constantly challenged while in the school.

Find out if your school has a system to identify and control access to visitors. If it doesn't, get to a parent advisory committee meeting and request that a system be in place as soon as possible.

Injuries on the Playground

In Canada, injuries kill more people between the ages of one and twenty than all other causes of death combined. They are the leading cause of death among children up to age nine. The sad part is that almost all injuries can be prevented. In 1996, poisoning, falls, and automobile accidents accounted for almost 70 percent of injury-related deaths in children and youth.

Fortunately, not all incidents result in the death of a child, although many are quite serious. Did you know that more than 28,500 children require medical attention each year due to playground injuries, and almost 2,000 of them require hospitalization? Almost 70 percent of injuries on playgrounds are caused by falls off climbers, swings, and slides. We expend huge effort in preventing children from climbing the furniture and counters at home, then allow them to climb to great heights on the playground.

Parents should teach their children that safety on the playground applies when they are at school as well as when they are with you at the park. Safekids Canada provides some good rules for kids to follow on their website (www.safekidscanada.ca).

- Wait your turn.
- Go down the slide sitting on your bottom, and don't climb up the slide while another child is going down.
- Sit down on swings; never stand.
- Walk around the bottom of slides.
- Keep away from swings when other children are using them.
- Do not go on equipment that is meant for older children. (Parents should clearly point out what is safe and unsafe for their child's age and development level.)

Most accidental injuries that happen at school occur during the lunch hour. The most common injuries are sprains, twisted ankles, and fractures. These are usually related to sports activities played during break time. In-class injuries include burns, cuts, and scrapes.

Injuries are almost always preventable, and schools can initiate plans that can practically make their schools injury-free. The first line of defense is adequate adult supervision for all activities, recess, and lunch breaks. Adult monitors are necessary wherever there are children. Although peer-related monitors are effective in some situations, adults who are fully trained in first-responder first aid are essential in being able to predict dangerous conduct and in treating injuries quickly.

School Bus Safety

School buses and their safety have been topics of concern for parents for years. It is hard to understand why children are required to wear seat belts on almost every other motor vehicle but not on a school bus.

This is the rationale. School buses have been designed to protect their passengers by using the "compartmentalization system." This system professes to confine children within the padded compartment in the event of a crash. Buses' high-backed seats are anchored to the floor, stuffed with energy-absorbent material, and are positioned close together to create these compartments.

Transport Canada claims that in the event of a crash, traveling by school bus is the safest form of transportation for kids. Children are more at risk of traffic-related injuries while they are getting on and off the bus than while actually riding it. However, there are other risks to school bus safety that parents need to be concerned about.

Children are being bullied, assaulted, and sometimes injured while riding the bus. Some school buses will carry upward of thirty children at one time and often the only adult is the driver, who is busy controlling the vehicle. This leaves children vulnerable to bullies, injury, or even accidental death, as in the tragic case of four-year-old Allyceea Ennis, killed while riding a school bus to daycare. While the cause of her death is still unknown, there is evidence of pressure to her neck. It is believed that she fell off her seat, her balaclava catching on the seat in the process, and that she was strangled. School buses were designed for older children, not for toddlers, who need to be restrained in their seats for safety.

Since the tragic loss of Allyceea, the Ontario government is reviewing ways to improve safety on school buses, but recognizes that their findings will not be automatically adopted by other provincial governments.

If your children ride a school bus, there are ways to stay safe. Again, Safekids Canada provides a comprehensive list for kids.

- Be a few minutes early for the bus, and don't run after one.
- Walk on sidewalks facing approaching traffic.
- Take five giant steps back when the school bus is approaching.
- Establish eye contact with the bus driver and other drivers before crossing the street.
- Stay at least five giant steps away from the front, side, and back of a school bus.
- Do not attempt to pick up anything that you drop near or under the bus.
- Use the handrail as you walk up the steps.

- Take your seat immediately and remain seated throughout the ride.
- Respect other passengers. The bus ride is not the time to play.

These are some ways that your kids can increase safety on and near the school bus. You should also ride the bus with your children at least once to get a better idea of what they are facing along the way. Get to know the bus driver. Let them know if you have any concerns for your child's safety while he's in their care.

Discipline at School

In January 2004, the Supreme Court of Canada upheld but amended Section 43 of the Criminal Code, otherwise known as the "spanking law." I was asked to appear on a national news show to talk about the subject. I was familiar with the law, since I had used its authority many times while working as a cop. The following is just one example.

One night while on patrol I received a call to attend a family dispute—a child wanted to charge her father with assault. The twelve-year-old daughter had been out of control for some time. She was using drugs and alcohol, had total disregard for the house rules, brought dangerous people into the home, stole, cheated, and lied to every member of her family. She was heading down a very dangerous path, and her parents were frustrated and scared.

On that night, an argument escalated when the girl threw a large glass bowl at the family dog because it was barking, narrowly missing it. The father stood up from the kitchen table and grabbed his daughter by the arm. He led her into her bedroom and forcefully sat her on the edge of her bed. He did not injure her or cause any bruising. He used just enough force to lead her away from the kitchen where he felt she could become more dangerous. He told her that she was to stay in her room until she cooled off and they could talk further. The rest of the family agreed with his actions and supported him—they all feared for their safety at times when this girl became enraged.

The girl called the police, and got me.

I arrived at the home and heard both sides of the story. The two could not agree on anything except for the events that night which made it obvious to me they were both being truthful. The girl admitted to throwing the bowl at the dog but said that her dad had no right to grab her by the arm and push her onto her bed. She wanted him charged with assault. The father sat waiting to be arrested because he too believed that he could not physically discipline his child.

You can imagine their surprise when I explained that he was completely within his rights to physically discipline his daughter and that he had not assaulted her. The girl argued for a while, trying to convince me to drag her dad off to jail. She was not willing to take responsibility for her actions at all. The call ended with both sides cooled off and more informed. The girl, however, grew up to be a violent and dangerous person, someone whom police came to know well.

Section 43 did not end at discipline at home by parents; it also included the right to physical discipline at school by teachers or the principal—that is, until January 2004. Until that date, according to the nineteenth-century law still in place, teachers could physically discipline a child at school as long as they did not cause any physical injuries. This could and did include a slap on the back of the hand, a ruler to the bottom, and once I recall a Ping-Pong paddle being hit across my friend's head for poor penmanship. Her mother, by the way, did nothing about it.

I would be surprised if today's parents would sit by and allow a school to apply corporal punishment. Most schools have not used their authority under Section 43 for many years. Educators understand that violence used for correction only breeds more violence.

Section 43 was upheld, but has more reasonable guidelines. It now only gives authority for parents to use "reasonable corrective force" with children between the ages of two and twelve. No instruments or objects can be used, and the discipline must be "minor corrective force of transitory or trifling nature."

As for teachers, they can use limited force to restrain unruly children—for example, to break up a fight—but they cannot hit them. It is a fine line to draw between the rights and needs of children. Children should not be subjected to corporal punishment at school—period. That in itself is barbaric. However, teachers need to know they will not be punished if they need to step in to break up a fight between kids. I am certain that if a teacher stood by and allowed a fistfight, and one child got seriously injured, that teacher's neglect in protecting the children would be headline news.

It is reasonable and necessary to allow teachers to touch kids if it means protecting them from harm. As a parent, you may need to physically pull your dangling child from monkey bars that she refused to climb down from herself. You also need to be sure that you will not end up in jail for physically removing your child from harm's way. If we go so far as to restrict all reasonable actions, we will open up our children to a variety of dangers.

Family Violence Goes to School

You may be shocked to learn that many of the students attending your child's school survive in violent and abusive homes. At times, this violence can be brought directly to the hallways of the school. You need to find out what policies and procedures your school has in place to deal with domestic disputes, custody issues, and other family situations that have the potential to explode into violence on school property.

We were told as cops that the most dangerous type of call was the domestic dispute. There are usually highly charged emotions of fear and rage, there may be weapons, and children are often involved. Every domestic dispute has the potential to become deadly.

But just because we call it a domestic dispute does not mean it always remains in the home. Schools need to prepare for the potential threat of family violence within the school. They need to have a critical incident response plan in place that focuses on keeping all children safe from violence.

Ask your principal,

- Do you have a plan in place that deals with family violence in the school?
- What do you tell students to do if they witness a family dispute in the hallways?
- Are you aware of any families that attend the school who may be at risk of domestic violence?
- Would you inform parents of these risks?
- Do you keep personal records private?

Teach your children to come to you if they witness anything that makes them feel uncomfortable or scared, or if they have a friend they believe is being hurt or abused. You may need to take action to ensure that their friend is safe and call the police to investigate further.

If this happens, be sure to recognize that it is not easy for your child to let you know about his concerns. He will feel a strong sense of loyalty to his friend in need. Praise him for telling you, and reassure him that you will help to make sure his friend is not hurt any longer.

Be sensitive to your child. If the authorities determine that the other child needs to be protected, and as a result is removed from the family, your child may be feeling very guilty and responsible for causing the breakup.

Children and adults often fear making a mistake by telling authorities about possible abuse. "What if I am wrong?" "What will happen to the children and the family?" "Will I ever see my friend again?" These are all valid questions, and they go far to explain why abuse often continues in families and communities long after the first suspicions are raised. The fact is, these concerns should all take second place to your concern for the child who may be living in an abusive situation.

Be confident that it is your responsibility to report your concerns, not investigate them. I can't stress enough the importance of taking this very difficult step. I assure you, by getting involved, even by making an anonymous report, you are not only doing the right thing—you may be saving a child's life.

School Trips

I loved school field trips when I was a kid. Even if my class headed out the door to a neighboring park to collect colorful maple leaves for a fall art project, it was a real treat to break free from the classroom and learn in a new environment. School trips are popular and effective in making a learning experience memorable. However, taking the time to plan for the unexpected can make the difference between a successful field trip and a tragic one.

The very best approach to field trips is to plan ahead and book the time off work so you can go with your child. Schools usually welcome parents as extra supervision, and school-aged children still want Mom or Dad around as much as possible. Your child will be ecstatic if you are able to go on the trip. I remind myself often that before I know it, I will be begging for their attention! Field trips can be a great way to spend memorable time with your kids in their world, and it can be quite enlightening to see your child interact with his peers.

If you can't be present, be sure that you take extra steps to get the details of the trip well in advance. As well as inquiring about the educational value of the trip, you should ask the teacher the following questions.

- What is the exact time of departure and return?
- How will the children be transported? Is it by school bus or parent drivers? Do all parents have proper safety belts and restraints in place?
- How many adult supervisors will be going? How many children?
- What activities will the children participate in?
- Are there any hazards the teacher needs to be cautious of? Do you need to discuss them ahead of time with your child?

- How much time does the teacher take discussing the safety rules with the children before the trip?
- What plan does the teacher have in place if a child becomes lost or injured?
- Is the teacher certified in Emergency First Aid in case a child is injured?
- Does the teacher have all the information needed to contact you immediately if there is an emergency?
- Does the teacher have a recent picture of your child that can be used to locate him if he becomes lost?

You should always submit a recent color photo of your child to her teacher at the start of each school year. Write your child's name, weight, and height on the back. These photos should be brought by the teacher on any school outing. If a child becomes lost or separated, the photo will assist officials in locating the child quickly.

In Canada, winter field trips often revolve around skiing, skating, sledding, tobogganing, snowboarding, or other snow-related sports. After all, Canada's winters produce great snow conditions from coast to coast, and some of the best outdoor opportunities are found in the northern Rocky Mountains. However, winter trips can be risky. According to the Canadian Safety Council, more than 40 percent of injuries sustained on field trips took place during a skiing or snow-related trip. This is typically due to lack of expertise, supervision, and inherent risk in the activity itself.

As a result of these alarming statistics, school board officials and schools are being forced to look closer at the risks that come with a chosen field trip activity. If the risks are high, as they are in skiing, they may need to complete a thorough risk assessment prior to being approved.

This was not done in February 2003, when seven students from an Alberta private school were killed by a massive avalanche while on a school ski trip near Rogers Pass, British Columbia. This was one of the worst school outdoor accidents in Canadian history. The sense of loss was tremendous, not only because of the young people who died, but because the tragedy could have been prevented.

The result was a full-scale investigation into the process that the school had gone through to determine the risk of this particular trip. The report suggested that both the school and parents had contributed to the deaths of these teenagers. The school had not properly assessed or managed the risks associated with the trip, and the parents were complacent in signing consent forms without becoming fully informed.

To be sure that your child will be safe on a school trip, find out all the details relating to the trip beforehand, ensuring that a risk management policy is in place and has been used. If you have concerns, investigate further. If your concerns are not resolved, do not give your child permission to go. Instead, plan a special day that she will enjoy to help her accept that she is not going on the field trip with her classmates.

Field trips can be a fantastic way for teachers and students to learn about their communities and subjects of special interest and value. They certainly add a fresh approach to daily school work. Accidents and other tragedies on field trips can be completely eliminated when preparation and the proper plan have been put in place.

Unsafe Practices

Although they mean well, teachers and school administrators sometimes implement activities and plans that are not in the best interests of safety. This is usually due to the fact that parents and teachers alike prefer to see everyone associated with school as equally invested in the safety of all kids. But this is not always the case.

Schools contain not only fantastic, caring, loving families, but also some violent, abusive, addicted, dangerous families, not to mention the potential intruder who has no business wandering the hallways in the first place.

I have put together a list of the top four unsafe practices that I see on a regular basis in schools. If you see these in your school, I suggest that you bring the potential risks to the attention of your child's teacher at once. There is a balance that must be struck between allowing for an open learning environment and becoming paranoid. Consistent, realistic assessment of potential threats will help you strike that balance.

1. Labeling belongings. I discussed this point in chapter two, but I am bringing it up again because it is one of the most common mistakes that schools continue to make. If you write your child's name on any item that is visible to a bystander, you could be helping a predator gain the trust of your child. Never label your child's belongings with his full name, phone number, and address—regardless of what your school tells you.

2. Visible information sheets. Never fill out a publicly accessible "family information" sheet that asks for personal information. I have seen such sheets posted in highly visible hallway areas that request information such as the child's and parents' names, home address, phone number, who usually picks them up and where. This information is ostensibly needed by the teacher and other parents in the class. For obvious reasons, though, giving this kind of information to others is unnecessary and risky. The school office has your address; the rest of the class doesn't need it. You likely don't know every parent in your child's class—not to mention everyone who happens to walk down the hallways!—and therefore should not assume they are all as safe as you are.

3. Public lists of students who wish to babysit. Many schools compile lists of kids who have participated in a babysitter training program and are looking for jobs. Kidproof Canada is the largest provider of babysitter training in the country. We tell our students they should never, under any circumstances, babysit for someone they do not know, let alone make their names and phone numbers widely available. This is breaking a strict rule. I once challenged a school official about making these names public, and was told quite sincerely that the secretary only gave out the names to "other parents from the school." I didn't realize that the test of dangerousness was if your child attended that school of over 400 children! Common sense tells us this is no guarantee of safety: we would be hard pressed to find a random group of upwards of 800 adults (two parents for each child) and not find at least one violent, potentially dangerous individual.

Parents who are looking for babysitters also need to do their homework and make sure the person they hire will be a safe, responsible caregiver for their child. Lists published by schools have the implied endorsement of the school. But just because a young person has taken and passed a babysitting course does not mean that he or she will be a great babysitter. You need to hire babysitters you know to be safe, reliable, and trusted. Talk to your co-workers, friends, and neighbors to see if they recommend anyone. Then be sure to meet, interview, and make your own judgment about whether the babysitter fits your needs before hiring her.

4. Dismissing children from class without supervision. At the end of the day, kids are ready for a change of scenery and are eager to get out of school. Many run from class to the playground or into their parents' arms. As kids get older and have learned safety rules such as "Never go anywhere with anyone without asking permission first," they can start to enter and exit the school on their own. However, I continue to see very young children, four and five years old, wandering out of class toward the outside doors alone, unsupervised and vulnerable. Parents need to pick their children up directly from the supervision of the teacher, not wait for them to come to the front of the school alone—schools are not inherently safe places. Teachers should not compromise the safety of these young kids. They should make sure that every child makes a safe transition to parents, to another adult who is authorized to pick the child up, or to the school bus.

Teachers, principals, and most parents have the same goals. All of them wish for the children in their care to grow up strong, healthy, wise, caring—and safe. Schools in Canada are, for the most part, fairly safe. We are not immune to the horrific tragedies that we read about almost daily among our neighbors to the south, but thankfully Canada does not have the same overpopulated, inner-city, gun- and gang-infested schools that are plaguing America. Canadian parents still need to be vigilant when it comes to their child's safety at school, and to recognize that there is no such thing as a completely safe school.

Chapter Nine

The Know-It-All Years: Talking to Your Teens, Keeping Them Safe

Now that my daughter is a teenager, she seems to be so much more secretive. When she was a little girl, we used to spend so much time together and now all she wants to do is hang out with her friends and listen to music. There are always boys calling her and she goes out every weekend. I don't know what she does when she is out and I am worried that she is either doing something illegal, or that she is not safe.

When asked the question, What hazards do you think teens face today?, parents and teenagers will have somewhat different answers. What parents may feel is a serious risk, teenagers are not too concerned about. What teenagers consider a risk to their safety, parents may never have considered or even known about. Your concerns will also depend on whether you have a daughter or a son. As well, you may be concerned that your child will become involved in criminal activity of some kind, whether through drug use, violence against others, theft, or even some form of sexual harassment or assault.

But I have some great news, something that most parents with teenagers forget. Even though your child may have turned into a rebellious teenager, you still have more control over his safety and his actions than you realize. It is true that teenagers need independence and the freedom to make choices so that they can become effective adults, but they still rely on you, their parent, for guidance, direction, and yes, approval. Just as they have since they were babies. And while they might tell you they can take care of themselves just fine, thank you, the truth is that you still play a crucial role in keeping your teens safe and helping them through the turbulent years of young adulthood.

As your children grow older and move beyond babyhood into childhood, into the narcissistic tweens and finally the argumentative teens, your focus on their personal safety changes. Your worries begin with childhood injury and abduction, and shift in the teen years to drugs, violence, and crime. Many people believe that as children grow, so does the seriousness of the dangers they face. For the most part, the seriousness remains the same; only the types of risk change.

What is frustrating is that for a dozen years or more, you have been the sole protector of your child. You have made all decisions that could affect her safety, paid close attention to her friends, and only allowed a select group of people that you knew and trusted into your family. So far, so good.

Then, almost overnight, your teenager decides she wants to make her own decisions—about almost everything. She wants to choose her own friends and begin to seek freedom and privacy when spending time with girlfriends or boyfriends. It is natural for parents to panic at the sudden loss of control. After all, no one consulted you about the change of rules!

But you probably remember what it was like to be a teenager, the things you did, the ways in which you rebelled, the things you were afraid of. And though times may have changed considerably, many of the fundamental fears that you had as a teenager remain constant today. The difference is in the methods used to access and harm teenagers.

The Internet has allowed predators to communicate with teenagers who in the past would have been beyond reach. Teenagers are particularly at risk of being seduced and lured away by a predator through online relationships. One U.S. study concluded that 26 percent of kids between the ages of nine and fifteen went to meet a friend whom they met online, without their parents' permission. So kids either don't know the rules, or don't understand the serious-ness of the threat.

There is a fantastic online Internet safety resource, which was developed by the National Center for Missing and Exploited Children in the U.S., for parents, children, and educators. They offer in-depth and effective interactive lessons that can be used in schools or in the home. These lessons target youth between the ages of five and seven-teen. The site also shows results from several surveys they have con-ducted, and reports based on interviews with kids and teens. I recommend you take a look at their website (www.netsmartz.org) for some insightful reading and information.

In one particular study, NetSmartz spoke to children ranging in age from ten to seventeen about forming close relationships with individuals whom they first met online. Their findings will help give you further insight into what your teenager may be doing online.

About 14 percent of youth reported that they had formed close friendships with people they first met online; 2 percent evolved into romances.

Teenage girls from fourteen to seventeen were about twice as likely to form close online relationships than tweens (ages ten to thirteen). This may be due to the fact that older teens are afforded more freedom and independence and have more opportunity to use the Internet. It is clear that teens who spend a lot of time online are also more likely to form close relationships developed over the Internet.

Their study appeared to show that all teenagers, both boys and girls, with high levels of parent-child conflict, low parent-child communication, feelings of vulnerability, depression, or a sense that their parents did not pay enough attention to where they were or with whom, were much more likely to form online relationships. Low self-esteem, depression, and loneliness were also linked to a tendency to seek out online relationships.

It must come as no surprise that the best way to protect your teenager from seeking outside acceptance, love, and attention is to be sure that you are keeping the lines of communication open at all costs. Your teen needs to know you will be there to celebrate their victories, commiserate over their defeats, and be there to talk when they encounter an upsetting or troubling situation. Studies prove over and over that youth with high levels of positive communication with their parents are less likely to seek advice and direction from others. These are safer kids.

Risks for Your Daughters

As my children are both boys, I admit there are times, as I watch the oodles of teenage girls parade through my house, desperately seeking the attention of my teenage son, that I empathize with parents of daughters. And, as a police officer, I investigated many cases that combined teenage girls, crime, victimization, and violence. There are unique risks that come with being female in Western society. But if your daughter learns to make safe choices as a teen, she will continue to be safe throughout her life. If you have not yet begun to provide her with the principles and tactics that will keep her safe, now is the time to start.

Parents of teenage daughters most often fear sexually motivated crimes. Crimes such as sexual assault and abduction, as well the possibility that their daughter will contract a sexually transmitted disease, top most parents' list of worries. Consider these Canadian statistics.

- 54 percent of sexual assaults reported to the police involve girls under the age of eighteen.
- Half of all Canadian women have experienced at least one act of sexual or physical violence since the age of sixteen.
- 34 percent of all sexual assaults reported in 2000 had female victims between the ages of twelve and seventeen.
- 24 percent of women have experienced rape or coercive sex, and 17 percent have experienced incestuous sexual assault of some description.
- Girls are two to three times more likely to experience sexual abuse than boys.

- 77 percent of all females were victimized (either sexually or physically or both) by someone they knew.

Although these statistics are alarming, what should stand out for parents is that violence is most often perpetrated by acquaintances or boyfriends of your daughter rather than by complete strangers. The risk of sexual assault to your daughter by someone she knows is far greater than you may think.

- Four out of five female undergraduates reported that they had been victims of violence in a dating relationship. Of that number, 29 percent reported incidents of sexual assault.
- 60 percent of Canadian college-age males report that they would commit sexual assault if they were certain they would not be caught.
- 31 percent of sexual assaults occur in dating and acquaintance relationships.
- 20 percent of Toronto secondary school students reported that they had experienced at least one form of assault in a dating relationship.
- In a Canadian study, 25 percent of all female post-secondary students in 1993 had been physically and/or sexually assaulted by a male date or boyfriend.
- In the same study, one in five male students surveyed said that forced intercourse was all right "if he spends money on her," "if he is stoned or drunk," or "if they had been dating for a long time."
- In 51 percent of all incidents of dating violence reported by Canadian women, the perpetrator was under the influence of alcohol.

How can you prevent your daughter from becoming a statistic? The first thing you have to accept is that your daughter, because she is female, is a target. But being a target doesn't have to equal becoming a victim.

As a police officer, I investigated countless sexual assaults of teenage girls. The severity of these assaults varied from an unwanted kiss to penetration. There was only one common factor that linked almost all of these cases. Again and again I heard statements like "I knew something was wrong," or "I had an awkward feeling about him, that I shouldn't trust him."

Unfortunately, many young girls learn to dismiss those early doubts. Yet those doubts are in fact their natural defense system, their instincts. If they do not trust their instincts and pay attention to the warning signs that cause them to feel uncomfortable, they will end up placing themselves in dangerous situations.

Why do girls (and some women) dismiss their instincts? Perhaps the most common reason is that girls have been taught, from an early age, not to be rude or unfriendly. Girls may also want to be liked, sometimes to the point of being desperate for acceptance by men or peers. Sometimes embarrassment—not knowing how to say no because it's just so awkward—is the simple reason for ignoring the warning signs. Teenagers with consistently low self-esteem and negative self-image are particularly at risk of poor decision making, resulting in increased risk.

As your daughter grows older and more independent, she will have to trust her own instincts and intuition more than ever. Encourage her to do so, and praise her when you see her making wise and safe choices for herself. She can rely on her instincts to protect her, as she has relied on you in the past.

The abusive and dangerous boyfriend

The number of girls who report being victimized by either a casual dating relationship or by a steady boyfriend is alarming. It is estimated that one out of every three females has been a victim of physical, emotional, or sexual abuse by a partner, at some time in their lives. It is likely that you know someone who has experienced violence in a dating relationship.

Parents need to understand and accept that if your teenage

daughter has fallen in love with a boy, he will come first. She will consider his feelings before yours, and often before her own. Young love is very powerful and persuasive. It can be a time in your daughter's life when she learns about her sexuality, her self-worth, and ultimately her limits. It can be a positive experience that will help your daughter's self-esteem thrive, or it can be the beginning of a long road of questioning her self-worth, and struggling with self-image and independence.

The success of the romantic relationships in your daughter's teen years can be pivotal in her future growth. This is not to say that one bad relationship will set her on a chain of dangerous and abusive boyfriends, but teaching your daughter to set and defend her limits will help dissuade her from taking chances.

It is not just teenage girls who fall madly, deeply, and blindly in love; boys can be equally affected by the love bug. But it would be false to say that parents of sons and daughters have the same things to fear when they consider what might happen when their offspring enter a relationship. Statistics tell us that males are by nature more violent than females. I apologize for having to make this generalization, but it's necessary for a realistic look at dating violence. Gavin de Becker, author of the *The Gift of Fear*, states: "Men of all ages and in all parts of the world are more violent than women. When it comes to violence, women can proudly relinquish recognition in the language because here at least, politically correct would be statistically incorrect."

Studies conducted on dating and violence clearly indicate that males and females use violence in relationships differently. Males are more likely to use violence to control their girlfriends, whereas females are more likely to use it against themselves or in self-defense. This does not mean there are no violent women in the world: there most certainly are. Let's face it: everyone is capable of violence, given the right situation and circumstances, whether they are motivated by power, control, criminal intent, or self-defense. Women *can* be violent, and sometimes are. However, it is statistically more likely that the violent partner in a relationship will be male.

The emotional investments that teenage girls make in their romantic relationships are colossal. However, young love can become less a dream than a nightmare for many teenagers and their families. An obsessive, possessive, and overly jealous boyfriend, coupled with young love, can be a deadly combination. But violence in relationships does not happen after one date. Gaining control is a gradual process that occurs when a young man does the following: diminishes his girlfriend's self-confidence by making belittling or insulting comments; isolates his partner from her friends and family by demanding her undivided attention and perhaps vilifying others in her life; and tries to persuade his girlfriend to believe that she would be nothing without him. These are controlling, manipulative behaviors that become worse over time.

It's important to understand that teenage girls who become involved in abusive and dangerous relationships can be from wealthy, educated, and loving families just as often as from dysfunctional, violent, and abusive families. Resist generalizing about who may be a victim—there is no stereotypical victim.

Likewise, there is no stereotypical abuser. Of course, there are factors that may increase the likelihood of someone becoming abusive, but do not fool yourself into thinking that abusers are always obnoxious, vulgar, and offensive—or that they must be fully grown adults before they can do serious harm. Violence can be learned by anyone who has had the misfortune of being exposed to it, and an abuser can become a practiced hand at an alarmingly precocious age.

If your daughter is in a possessive and/or abusive relationship, she may not confide in you. In fact, she will likely do everything she can to keep it from you until she can no longer handle it herself. Unfortunately, it may be difficult for you to spot the warning signs by watching her boyfriend, since he will almost certainly be charming and polite—a great guy—to you. Only the most blatant forms of abuse will be evident to an outsider like you.

Instead of looking to her boyfriend for clues, pay close attention to your daughter and any changes in her behavior. If there is a problem, there will be clear indicators early on. Don't wait for her to come to you; take initiative and look for the warning signs that will help you protect your daughter. The following story illustrates what I mean about warning signs. See if you spot the moments when an intervention should have been made.

A mother called me a while ago because she had become very concerned about her daughter, Charlene, and her daughter's boyfriend, James. When her daughter first met James, she was fifteen years old and he was seventeen. From the start, it was obvious to her mother that Charlene had a serious crush.

Her mother met James the first night that he came to visit Charlene. He seemed respectful, polite, and confident. She knew her daughter well, and could see why she was attracted to him.

The two began to date, and after several months her mother was certain that the two had become sexually active. Although Charlene had just turned sixteen, her mother understood that she was in love with James and so instead of trying to make her daughter slow the relationship down, she encouraged her to use birth control consistently and wisely. She believed that by trying to stop the activity she would only cause conflict between her and her daughter, so she decided to accept James into the family and often invited him to family functions and even on vacations.

Her mother liked James and felt she could trust him. He was always attentive to Charlene and seemed to be as committed to her as she knew her daughter was to him. Charlene even started to take on James's gestures, likes, and dislikes, which her mother found amusing. She seemed to be much happier when she was with him.

But Charlene began to change. Her mother noticed that she was devoting all her time and attention to pleasing James, and was not spending much time with her friends anymore. Their usual mother-and-daughter chats were less frequent and more strained. But her mother brushed off her concern and tried to remember what it was like to be in love as a teenager and how all-consuming the feelings can be.

Her concerns resurfaced when she saw that Charlene started to fear rejection from James. She seemed to be obsessed with worry that he was cheating on her, and that he did not find her attractive anymore. Charlene began to diet and exercise excessively, and lost a tremendous amount of weight. She would not make any decisions without his approval. She often said that she worried James did not love her as much as she loved him.

The shared family outings had stopped, since every invitation was met with another excuse. Her mother didn't see much of James anymore, and Charlene explained that they preferred to be alone. It was obvious that she was keeping secrets from her mother. If her mother said anything even remotely negative about James, Charlene would strike back and adamantly defend him. The communication between her and her mother had almost completely broken down.

Charlene's mother tried on many occasions to talk to her daughter, but got nowhere. Just before her seventeenth birthday, Charlene moved out of her family's home and in with James.

Her mother could not believe this had happened. She told me she feared that her daughter was being abused by James, either emotionally or physically. She had no other explanation for her daughter's withdrawal from her family and friends. It was clear that James wanted her to himself, and it appeared to this frightened parent that she had lost her daughter entirely. She was consumed with guilt over allowing the relationship to continue for so long.

It semed to this woman that everything had happened so quickly. But as she told the story, it became clear that her daughter's changes and distancing began subtly, and continued to build until she became completely absorbed with James and isolated from everyone else.

There were warning signs that, had they been addressed reasonably and swiftly, might have given Charlene the courage to stand up to James, and set clear boundaries for herself.

Look for early warning signs in your teen's relationships. Resist the temptation to justify any problems you see with excuses like "It is only teen love," "She needs her privacy," or "She needs more freedom." Above all, do not let fear of confrontation keep you from speaking to her.

Warning signs of abuse

The following are clear warning signs that your daughter may be in an abusive relationship or heading toward one. In general, they all point to a loss of confidence and self-esteem.

- She changes her style of clothing or hair, seemingly in response to her boyfriend's tastes or distastes.
- She has trouble making decisions for herself.
- She stops spending time with friends.
- She begins to show failing grades.
- She begins to use alcohol or drugs.

If you recognize these signs in your daughter, you will have to intervene as soon as possible. Even better is proactive education, essential in preventing future problems. Be sure to take the time to discuss each sign with your daughter, regardless of whether she is currently in a relationship.

The following list tells you what to look for in her boyfriend's behavior. By the time you are seeing these signs, the relationship has almost certainly become abusive, and it is crucial that you take action.

- He shows signs of jealousy and possessiveness.
- He yells, humiliates, insults, or swears at your daughter.
- He is responsible for spreading false and degrading rumors about her, and often tries to make her feel guilty.
- He pressures her into sexual activity or wants to make the relationship serious before she is ready.
- He begins to make all decisions and expects to be asked permission before she agrees to other activities.

- He isolates her from her friends or family, demanding her full attention as often as possible.
- There are rumors that he has abused other girls in the past.
- When confronted, he minimizes the accusation and blames the girl.

In the story with Charlene and James, her mother tried on several occasions to speak to her daughter about her concerns but was met with resistance each time. It was clear that she needed help getting through to her daughter and addressing the obvious warning signs that she was witnessing.

Instead of trying the same tactics that were obviously not working, Charlene's mother needed to seek outside help after the first few tries to communicate were met with resistance. There are now services in almost every community to assist in cases of domestic violence. Many local police departments and hospitals can put you in touch with a crisis center in your area. Do not make the dangerous mistake of thinking these services are only for "battered women." They are also there for teens at risk of emotional, physical, and sexual abuse. You do not have to wait until your daughter is a victim before you seek help.

Let's go back to Charlene's story for a moment. By the time her mother called the police, Charlene was seventeen, and in Ontario that's old enough to live on your own, which the police were quick to confirm. Charlene was too old to be legally forced to return home, and unless she herself made a report of physical abuse, or the mother was a witness to abuse, there was nothing the police could do.

The police did agree to check on Charlene, to see if she was safe and being provided for. What they found were two teenagers living in a low-income apartment with enough furniture and food to subsist. They talked to Charlene, who said that she was not afraid of James, and that it was her choice to live there. They suggested that she call her mother, then left.

Unfortunately, there is a distinct difference between believing that something is happening and *proving* it. The police had no grounds on which to pursue James.

When you confront your daughter about your concerns for her, do not force your opinions on her: she will only resist. Do not give her ultimatums such as telling her she cannot be part of your family as long as she is dating someone you do not approve of. Do not assist her boyfriend in making her feel she is truly alone. Likewise, however, do not allow her to think that her boyfriend has the right to abuse or degrade her.

Instead of trying to control your daughter, bolster her self-esteem by showing her your unconditional love. Tell her you are always there for her, regardless of whom she is dating. Tell her you do not approve of how her boyfriend treats her, and remind her that she is valuable, deeply loved by her family and friends, and worthy of being loved. Be a positive role model for her; she will learn from watching you set and defend your personal boundaries in your own relationships. Your teenage daughter will look to the adult women in her life for direction, guidance, and, most important, what is acceptable and appropriate in a relationship. A strong and safe teenage daughter has a mother who examines her own actions and reflects her self-esteem through positive, healthy relationships of her own.

As you face the task of helping your daughter overcome an abusive relationship, remember that you are not alone. There is a wealth of resources available for women and families today. Make use of it.

Violent behavior will not just go away. It will continue to increase in frequency and ferocity unless it is stopped. No matter how dedicated your daughter is to her boyfriend, no matter how much she loves him, she cannot and will not change him.

When the relationship ends

As the song goes, breaking up is hard to do. This is especially true if an obsessive, abusive, and possessive boyfriend is involved.

If your daughter has acknowledged she is in an abusive relationship, and is ready to break it off, it is crucial that she do so completely and finally. There is no room for gestures such as "let's just be friends" or "maybe we need a break for a while." All communication must stop, including phone calls, letters, or messages passed through common friends. If your daughter responds just once to a gesture, even something as simple as a wave from across the street, he will interpret this as an opportunity to re-enter her life. She may only be waving to be nice, but he will see it as a reason to hope for reconciliation.

If your daughter's ex-boyfriend does not respect her wishes to cease having contact with him, and he persists in trying to get in touch with her, it is important that you respond immediately. You will need to let everyone know that this ex-boyfriend poses a threat. Do not try keep it a secret. It is imperative that you inform your neighbors, the school, and other family members of the breakup; only in this way can all those who care about your daughter's safety be helpful in watching for warning signs and keeping her safe.

You will also need to contact the police.

In Canada it is a crime to repeatedly harass, make contact (either directly or indirectly), follow, watch, or threaten someone. It's commonly referred to as stalking, but in legal parlance it's known as criminal harassment and it's taken very seriously. Broken obsessive and possessive relationships can quickly turn violent and even deadly if action is not taken at the very start.

There are several ways that police can assist you in putting up legal protection for your daughter and your family. Each will depend on the evidence and specifics of the case, and not all will result in the arrest and criminal charge of the ex-boyfriend. It is important to understand, though, that *legal* protection does not equal *physical* protection.

The most common response from the police will be to issue a

restraining order against the offending party. A restraining order is a legal agreement and to breach it is a crime. Many cases of criminal harassment do settle down once a restraining order is in place. However, you should remember that an obsessive ex-boyfriend may be more concerned with seeing your daughter than with committing a crime. If you are considering a restraining order, realize that it is a *layer* of protection that confirms your daughter's desire to break off communication, but it will not physically protect her or your family.

It is true that there are tragic cases where harassment and domestic violence escalate to the point of murder. In some of those cases, restraining orders are in place and do not ultimately protect women from the men who are determined to destroy them. Yet it is still important to make the initial complaint. Names, addresses, and vehicles can be flagged by the police as a high risk of domestic violence and these can assist the police in attending to a call more quickly—if it ever comes.

Unfortunately, often the police are not called soon enough because the victim is afraid of causing her ex-boyfriend to be charged with a crime, or because she is afraid of confronting him in court. Keep in mind that criminal charges are not always the result of a criminal harassment investigation.

It is vital that you and your family seek outside help in dealing with a persistent ex-boyfriend and support your daughter through this very difficult test of strength. In order to truly be protected, she must completely remove herself from the relationship, heal from the wounds it has caused, and move on to find the relationship she deserves.

Girls who are violent

In 1997, Canadians were stunned when they learned of the brutal attack and murder of fourteen-year-old Reena Virk in Victoria, British Columbia. It was not only the death of such a young, vibrant girl that was so disturbing, but the fact that her tormentors were mainly other teenage girls.

Girl-on-girl violence became headline news and the statistics supported the dismaying claim. In 1997, Statistics Canada showed that crimes involving teenage girls were up 5 percent over the ten-year period between 1987 and 1997. In that period, 4,800 teenage girls were charged with violent offenses in Canada. This number is staggering, and would make anyone alarmed.

What is going on with girls anyway? Statistics have always proven in the past that males are inherently more violent than females, so why are so many teenager girls striking out in violent rages?

Let's look more closely at what's behind the statistics. Girls are becoming involved in more violent crimes; however, those crimes are usually less severe than those committed by their male counterparts. Two-thirds of the charges laid against girls in 1997 were for minor assaults. These can include hitting, shoving, or slapping, but otherwise not causing serious injury or bodily harm. Very serious assaults, such as the murder of Reena Virk, represented less than 1 percent of the violent charges laid that year.

I spoke to a group of teenage girls from a middle-class neighborhood in British Columbia. I asked them if they feared being assaulted by another girl. Astoundingly, their answer was yes!

Each one of these teenage girls admitted either to being a victim of assault or to knowing someone who had been. They explained that, from their point of view, it seems that girls are fighting more than ever and there is no hiding from the potential violence. Girls are targeted not only for their actions, as you might think, but also by their association with others. High schools are densely populated these days, some with over a thousand students enrolled. You might think, as I did, that a large school would mean that anyone could blend in and avoid being singled out as a target. Makes perfect sense to me. But the girls were unequivocal about this. They explained that, in order to blend in, you have to belong to some group or you will be obviously different. But once you belong to a group, any group, you will have enemies. It is just that simple.

So now what? Do you expect that your daughter will eventually be in a fight and just hope for the best? Do you teach her to fight, enroll her in boxing lessons, self-defense, karate? Maybe just take her out and home-school? If I were a parent of a teenage daughter, I might consider all of the above. But my knowledge of crime and criminality prevents me from following my initial knee-jerk reaction and forces me to look at the reasons behind the violence in order to prevent it rather than run from it.

First we have to understand what provokes a fight. Often for girls, it is rumors, competition over boys, jealousy, and pride. It is important for teenage girls to secure their position in their peer groups and if they become the target of rumors, they feel the need to defend their reputation, which can result in physical violence.

Furthermore, girls are more likely to become violent and aggressive toward others if they are from violent homes, have been physically, sexually, or emotionally abused, or if they have little parental attention, support, or guidance. Any attention they can get, even negative, is worthwhile to them, and violence is a sure attention-getter.

To help your daughter remain free from violent attack—and to keep her from becoming violent—go back to the basic task of staying connected, and open to communicating with her. Schools across the country are taking seriously the problem of teen violence, and to deal with the problem many schools have implemented effective, long-term anti-violence and anti-bullying programs.

Some schools have initiated tougher penalties, zero tolerance, and many have the police walk the hallways and grounds on a regular basis. Some schools have resorted to supplying small offices to the police so they can write incident reports while at the school.

Many initiatives, with the exception of anti-violence education, are reactive at best. But simply initiating tougher penalties through the school community and law enforcement will not solve the problem.

What educators need to do is get out and become part of their school communities. The principal needs to be the leader of their community—the school. He or she should walk the hallways with the kids, take the time to know what the kids are interested in, what groups control different areas of the school, if there are signs of gang activity or drugs. Educators need to communicate with the kids and realize that the students can teach them a lot about what is happening outside their office doors each day.

The key is to encourage the parents, students, educators, and law enforcement to talk together on a regular basis, not just when an incident arises. Give the kids a voice, encourage them to become positive and effective leaders, and show every child that he or she is valuable, vital, and loved.

Risks for Both Genders: Alcohol and Crime

When my first son was still a baby, I said, on more than one occasion, "I could never be angry or disappointed with him. I can't imagine him ever doing anything wrong." Yes, I admit I said it, because I actually believed that I could "understand" him. For several years I lived with the illusion that my son was impervious to the dark side, resistant to the defiance and manipulation that I was warned came with the teen years. That is, until he turned thirteen, and the refrain of "Mom, you just don't understand" began to get past my own resistance.

What came next was worse. "Mom, nothing bad is going to happen to me." Now, the average parent, hearing this statement, would likely be alarmed, but try to imagine what it was like for me, a cop and child-safety expert, to be blindsided by such a remark.

Let me try to paint a picture for you: There I stood in my kitchen, tired from a ten-hour shift on patrol, and drinking at least my thirteenth cup of coffee that day. My son, all of five feet, three inches, eighty-five pounds, and thirteen years, actually believed I was going to let him go to a party with his friends at a downtown underage club. This was the very same club I had attended countless times for complaints of violent assaults, weapons, drugs, fights, and every other disastrous midnight event imaginable.

I recall wondering if I had heard him right. All that passed my lips was "What???" It was only one word, but my tone and expression clearly said, You have got to be kidding. Never in a million years would I let you go to that place. Of course he persisted, and I resisted.

If, like many parents, you've done a great job of keeping your child safe from violence, it can be difficult to convince him that he is not invincible and there are real risks out there. What a terrible predicament to be in. Have you become the victim of your own success?

Only partially. I am not a strong proponent of scare tactics. I have found over and over again that they only succeed in giving someone a really interesting story to tell. As well, because incredibly dramatic stories usually are about relatively rare events, teens find them hard to relate to. After all, what are the chances that something so horrific could happen? If they can't relate to a story, if they can't see themselves in the same situation, they will not be able to learn from the mistakes of others.

So your job is clear. To get through to your son or daughter, you have to find a situation or story that is similar enough to your children and their environment that they can relate and understand the seriousness of the threat. If they can relate to it, they will learn from the outcome.

I decided it was time to talk to my son about drinking alcohol. Of course I had discussed drugs, alcohol, and violence in the past. But when he was sixteen, I learned that on some weekends he was going down to the beach and drinking with friends. He was not getting wiped-out drunk, but he was certainly taking part in the festivities.

I did not approve of his actions but decided to talk to him to see if I could get more information. He is, and always has been, an "easy interview"—his face and expressions give him away every time. We started to talk about what he and his friends did while they were at the beach, and he admitted that sometimes his friends drank too much and got "wasted." I could see that my son had genuine concern for his friends' well-being when they were drinking—not that he was a completely innocent bystander at all times.

I chose to talk to him about the dangers of drinking so much at such a young age. I knew that my son was very opposed to losing control, and that he felt strength in helping others; I used both of these to my advantage. I explained that drinking alters your perception and your actions, and that he would obviously lose control if he became drunk. If he were only with his close friends, that might not be much of a concern, but there were always others around that he didn't know well or trust. It was clear to him that he would become vulnerable.

I struck a nerve, so I went deeper. Aside from the fact that it was illegal for him and his friends to be drinking alcohol, did he know what to do to make sure that his friends were safe if they drank too much? He was unsure what I was talking about.

I explained that people who drink too much can pass out and, if they vomit while in the wrong position, asphyxiate themselves. In other words, they could choke and suffocate. He was not aware of such a thing. I explained that if a friend is very drunk and goes to sleep, he should ensure that she is lying on her side in the recovery position, not sitting up or lying on her back. He could save a life by doing this simple thing, I explained, but only if he was sober and in control himself.

He was empowered by the knowledge that he could help his friends in a time of need. I didn't focus on his participation in the drinking, although it was clear that I disapproved, but instead gave him solid and valid reasons to stay sober. I empowered him with knowledge that far outweighed his desire to become completely inebriated.

Wondering how the evening's argument over the underage club unfolded? As I said, he persisted, I resisted. He was angry, and thought that I was being a paranoid, overprotective cop, but I was confident in my decision and knew better. After all, it was still my job to protect him—as a mother, not as a cop.

Is my child going to become a teenage criminal?

As a police officer, I saw teenagers who had crossed the line, made bad choices, and were paying the consequences. I witnessed teenagers determined to continue on a path of destruction, obviously having no respect for others, and certainly none for themselves.

Contrary to what many people believe, these kids are not all from broken, dysfunctional families. Of course, some kids are placed on this dangerous path by their parents' own criminality and selfishness. These teens are victims of their parents' neglect and abuse, and come by their deviant behaviors honestly.

But, for most teens, criminal activity is not a natural progression. Most youth crime is committed by a small population of active criminals who offend and then reoffend. The majority of teens are likely to come into contact with police because they have gone to a noisy party that police have been called to, or for loitering or some minor mishap. Many teens have loving, caring, and well-educated parents who are eager to do everything it takes to keep their kids safe and out of trouble. If you are reading this book, you probably fit that description.

But sometimes, no matter what you do, no matter how much you talk to your kids and how clearly and confidently you set your limits, you'll find that your kids test them. Teens will break the rules in their efforts to gain more independence from you and acceptance from their peers. If you are among the parents who still believe that your child would never do anything wrong, please listen to this reality: your kids, too, will break your rules sometimes.

Hopefully, the rules they choose to break will be minor, and your children's actions will have little effect on their safety and that of others around them. Hopefully, they are ready for the freedom and independence that come with the teen years.

Tips from Expert Interviewers: How to Talk with Your Teen

Throughout this book, I've talked about the importance of "keeping the lines of communication open." This is a tall order, and sometimes not easy, especially when talkative children turn into secretive teenagers. It can be hard to know what questions to ask, or how to respond to your teens in conversation. But being able to talk to them, and knowing what they're up to, are genuinely important if you are going to continue to keep them safe, and if you want them to come to you when they are in trouble.

How can you know what your child is doing when he or she is no longer directly under your supervision? Teens are inherently private and guarded, often for good reason. And while it's tempting to want to know everything (particularly when your inquiries are met with vague or evasive explanations), you don't really need to know everything. Your teen still needs you to guide him, though, so you should know the big stuff, the major decisions, the vital choices that can affect their lives.

How do you find out what's really going on with your teen? Well, you likely have all the tools you need every time you sit down to dinner with your kids.

Yes, you heard right, there is a way to get vital information from your kids through conversation. I can't think of a better way to learn about your teens than to talk with them. But, to help you move beyond the standard "I don't know" from your teens, I'm going to pass on a few tips of the trade.

Police are, without a doubt, among the best communicators imaginable. Police must be skilled at listening, observing, and probing in order to find the truth in any situation. A criminal has nothing to lose, and everything to gain, by being untruthful to the police. But police are used to deceit, lies, and talking to unwilling participants. Skilled police officers can get to the truth quickly, effectively, and often without the participant even realizing that he's given himself away.

Police probe for the truth to investigate a crime: they need proof. You, the parent, need to find out the truth for other reasons: because you're concerned about your child's safety, or to get at the root of a problem. Sometimes this information is about a boyfriend or girlfriend, sometimes it is about drugs, alcohol, or other abuses, and sometimes it is about criminal activity and violence. But it is almost always about when you believe that they have done something wrong.

Parents are not police. They should never attempt to interview their children and teens as the police would. But some of the truth-finding methods that police use can also be very valuable in discovering if your child is at risk or heading in the wrong direction. You don't need to hook up a polygraph (lie detector) machine to your kids, nor do you need to make your conversations as official as interviews. All you need is to learn *how* to ask a question that will give you quality information, when to ask it, and what to do with the information you receive.

Remember I described my oldest son as an "easy interview"? Well, your son or daughter can be too, if you follow some simple guidelines and tips to forensic interviewing.

I know what you're thinking: it's difficult enough at times to get your teen to talk about his day at school in any great detail, so how are you ever going to get him to talk about something that is certain to get him into trouble.

It is easier than you think, but it doesn't happen all at once. Practice your communication skills in all types of scenarios, not just when you think your teenager has done something wrong. As you begin to get comfortable with the process, you'll start to rephrase your questions automatically. Always realize that open communication is essential in keeping your child safe and well protected. Becoming a skilled listener will help you get to the root of a problem that could be potentially dangerous and that your child is not open to discussing.

Consider this story:

Your daughter is out with her friends on a Saturday, hanging around the mall. You know all of her friends, and whom she is with. You are also familiar with the mall, and she has been there on many occasions. You don't feel there is any need to be concerned for her.

Later that afternoon, you get a call from the parent of one of your daughter's friends. She advises you that her daughter was caught shoplifting a t-shirt from a store in the mall. She suspects that your daughter was also involved and may have stolen something herself. She explains that the rest of the girls ran away before the security guard could catch them all. Your daughter has not arrived home yet.

As a parent, how can you find out if your daughter was involved, and, most important, if she too had shoplifted from the mall? You know she is likely to deny any involvement and will come up with an explanation. You don't have proof that she stole anything, but you are certain she was part of the crowd. As you wait for her to return home you need to prepare for the conversation.

You may feel angry, disappointed, and frustrated with your teen, and these feelings are okay. It is acceptable to be angry; after all, your daughter made a bad choice. But in order to get the truth from her, you are going to have to put the anger, disappointment, and frustration aside, at least at first.

TIP: People cannot lie to a friend as easily as they can to an enemy.

This is a true and guiding principle you will need to remember each time you seek to gain information from anyone, including your teen. People cannot lie to a friend, or they at least find it very difficult to do so. You may be thinking about the old cop shows on TV with the "good cop, bad cop" formula. It's not only entertaining to watch, but one thing usually holds true: the "good cop" eventually gets the information or confession.

Identify your goal

What is your goal in talking to your child? Is it to get proof or is it to get to the root of the problem? Will the answers you are looking for help you direct your child to a safer place and situation—or are you just being snoopy? If you have decided that as a matter of safety and guidance you need to know more about a situation, then continue. However, if you are just curious about what he does when you are not with him, and have no real concern for his safety, resist probing and give him the privacy he needs to grow.

In the case above with the daughter and shoplifting, you would need to determine not only if your teenager stole from the mall, but why. This would be a good reason to move forward with your questioning.

Set up the place to talk

Find a place in your home that is comfortable for talking. Do not place any objects between yourself and your daughter, since they will only act as supports for her to be dishonest. Sit next to each other on a sofa or on one side of a table, never across the table from each other. Remember the guiding principle that people can't lie to their friends as easily as they can to their enemy. So be sure to choose a non-confrontational and comfortable place to talk, where you will have few distractions.

Be sure not to use the same place each time that you decide to have a serious talk with your teen. If every serious conversation begins with sitting on the living room sofa, your son or daughter will quickly catch on to the pattern and become guarded before the conversation can even get started.

Get the story

The person who knows the most about the situation is your child. And though you probably know more than she thinks you do, there is no need to let on and show her all your cards from the start. Begin by letting your child do most of the talking, while you do most of the listening.

Begin the interview by asking your teen to tell you the story of what happened that day. A simple question will do, for instance, "So tell me what you did today at the mall?"

Your goal is to keep them comfortable, and talking. There are subtle ways that you can encourage conversation.

1. Provide positive reinforcement. If you find that during the story your teen seems to hesitate or wants to stop talking about a specific detail, try leaning in, smiling, or nodding. You can use words or phrases such as "Great," "Go on . . . ," "Sounds good . . . ,"

"And . . . ," "So. . . ." These small conversational gestures will usually be enough to make her continue, and give you more details.

2. Use the ten-second rule. People for the most part are uncomfortable with silence, especially during a close and serious conversation. They often feel compelled to fill in silence with further details or explanation. Even adults can get themselves into trouble with their uncontrollable need to avoid uncomfortable silence.

This compulsion to fill silence explains why silence can be very powerful to an interviewer. Use this power. If your child seems to have come to the end of a story, pause as if you are expecting more. Combine positive reinforcement with the ten-second rule: "So . . ." (allow ten seconds to elapse). It will be very difficult for your child to resist filling in the silence. Often the details that are obtained during this time are full of important information.

3. Watch for closed body language. Your teen will give you cues that she is uncomfortable with a topic, or simply not willing to discuss it. These can come in the form of nervous mannerisms, twitches, or "tics" of various kinds.

You know your child best and will probably identify a new movement quickly and accurately. I know when one of my sons is uncomfortable or being deceitful because he stares at the wall behind me as he talks. He has done this all his life, so when I see it now, I know what it means.

You can also determine if your child is uncomfortable by watching whether she seeks a safer place to talk. Often people will move or walk to a new position that places an object between them and you, such as the kitchen table. Take this as a sign that she feels the need to be more guarded and protected.

Some other body language that points to a person closing down or feeling uncomfortable about a topic is sitting with crossed legs, crossed arms, turning her body away from you, looking down, or leaning backward to create distance between you and her.

If you recognize any of these signs in your teen, you can either wait until the behavior goes away or, more effectively, try to make your son or daughter comfortable again by introducing a topic that you know is easy for him or her.

For example, in the shoplifting scenario above, let's say that your daughter is at the point in her story where her friend gets caught. At this point, she suddenly gets up to get a drink of water and stands with the table between you and her. The flow of the conversation has changed and suddenly stopped at her initiation. Her actions make it obvious that she is uncomfortable with telling you the rest of the story. You will need to make her comfortable again.

So, get a glass of water yourself and join her on the same side of the table and go back to a point in the story that she was comfortable discussing, such as when they were having lunch before the shoplifting incident. Encourage the story to continue again.

Is the Story True? Using the 30–50–20 Rule

You won't be able to tell 100 percent if your son or daughter is being truthful unless he or she comes right out and admits a wrongdoing. But if you maintain open lines of communication and connection with your child, and he trusts that you will treat him fairly, he is likely to tell you the truth. However, there are ways of knowing if he is holding something back, or not quite telling the story the way it happened.

A typical truthful story will break down as follows: about 30 percent will be background to the story, 50 percent will describe the actual event with details, and 20 percent of the story will be the conclusion. For example, a truthful statement about the shoplifting scenario may sound like this:

Jenny, Brenda, Jill, and I were at the mall today. We got there around eleven o'clock and the mall was pretty busy. We just hung around a bit and ran into a couple of guys from school—you know them, Brad and Mike. Anyway, we all hung around for a while, had some fries at the food court, and then Brad and Mike had to go. So Jenny, Brenda, Jill, and I decided to go to this really cool store. They have awesome clothes and Jill saw this t-shirt in the window that she really liked.

We all went to the store and Brenda and I were in the back of the store and Jill and Jenny were looking for the t-shirt on a rack. Then Brenda's cell rang and it was Brad. He was coming back to the mall to hang out and asked if we would meet him at the bus stop out front. Brenda and I decided to go to meet him and Jill and Jenny stayed in the store.

We left and waited for Brad. He got there about half an hour later and we went back into the mall to find Jill and Jenny. They said they were going to meet us at the food court but they never came. We waited forever for them. I called Jill's cell and her mom answered. She sounded really mad. She said that Jill was with her and that I was supposed to go right home.

I hung around for a couple more minutes and then Brenda, Brad, and I caught the bus home. That's it.

This is likely a truthful statement. This person spent about 30 percent of her time giving background, 50 percent was taken up by the actual story of being in the store with Jill and going to meet Brad, and about 20 percent of the story was conclusion. If my daughter told me this story, in this order, I would believe it to be truthful. However, I would be suspicious if the story unfolded like this:

Jenny, Brenda, Jill, and I were at the mall today. We got there around eleven o'clock and the mall was pretty busy. We just hung around a bit and ran into a couple of guys from school—you know them, Brad and Mike. Anyway, we all hung around for a while, had some fries at the food court, and then Brad and Mike had to go.

So Jenny, Brenda, Jill and I decided to go to this really cool store. Then Brad called Brenda and we went out to meet him at the bus stop. We just hung out and then I came home.

The second version of the story is probably a version that you can imagine hearing from your child. In assessing its truthfulness, I would look carefully at how far it is from the 30-50-20 rule: it is far too vague. If my daughter told me this story, I would spend a lot more time getting to the details.

Breaks in the story

This example not only illustrates one variant of the 30-50-20 rule, it also shows how easily someone can leave out large portions of a story, usually in attempts to avoid revealing her activities. Often teenagers will avoid explaining large sections of a story in hopes that you will not notice and will move on to another topic instead.

Of course, large breaks in the story do not in themselves point to untruthfulness, and can be attributed to the child not remembering the incident, being embarrassed to tell all the details, or assuming that you already know. If you feel they have left out large chunks of the story, you will need to probe a little deeper.

Offering too many details

On the flip side of being too vague, some people who are being untruthful will overcompensate and offer too many details about insignificant things. They are doing this because they know they are not telling the truth: they are not only trying to convince you, they are also trying to convince themselves.

This type of deceit can become very clear when you are in the first part of the interview and are encouraging your child to do all the talking. In the scenario above, if your daughter is spending a lot of time describing the t-shirt that Jill liked, or the entire play-by-play conversation with Brad on the cell phone, you should be suspicious and probe deeper.

Another Method: Repeating the Story Backward

An easy way to notice inconsistencies or gaps in a story is to ask your teen to tell you the whole story back to front.

Say something like this: "Tell me everything that happened from the time you arrived at the mall until you came home." She will tell you the story, and you can apply the 30-50-20 rule. If you feel there are gaps or unexplained details, or have the feeling that she is not being totally truthful, ask her to tell you the story a second time, but instead of starting from the time she arrived at the mall, to begin from when she came home, and work backward.

Say something like this: "Okay, so to be sure that I understand, what did you do right before you got home?" Prompt her to recall the story, but in reverse order.

The reason that people get caught in lies is that lies are not as easily stored in long-term memory as truth is. For example, if you lie about a situation that happened to you today, and ten years from now someone asks you to recall that same situation, you will not be able to remember exactly what you said unless you wrote it down. If you told the truth, and ten years later were asked about the same situation, you would likely be able to recall the events with relative ease and accuracy. It is very difficult to remember lies.

By asking your teen to tell her story backward, you will make it much more difficult for her to be untruthful. Telling the story backward does not bring out the truth, but rather alerts you to where the truthfulness is questionable, and lets you focus further discussion on that area.

Other Ways of Getting to the Truth

If you have spent time talking about the incident, used all of the tricks to encourage dialogue, and you are still not getting the answers you need, you will need to change your tactics and ultimately the direction of the discussion.

First, remind yourself of the goal of the interview. You are trying to find out if your teenager is at risk of harm, or in the case of this scenario, if she has committed a theft. What you should be most concerned about learning is *why* she did something dangerous or wrong in the first place. It is only after you learn what motivated her to act that you can make a plan to prevent it from recurring in the future.

You should not approach this discussion with your kids from a police perspective, with the ultimate goal of proving beyond reasonable doubt that it happened. Instead, you should encourage conversation and discussion with your teen, even when it relates to bad decisions on her part. You want to be sure she will come to you whenever she needs help—for any reason.

After your child has done all of the talking and her story has ended, it is your turn to talk. This is the time that you will do most of the talking and ask clarifying questions.

For this to work you will need to be sure that you do not confront, accuse, or demand the truth. Instead, discuss the situation, using some of the following guidelines.

Don't ask questions that will give one-word answers
Never ask a question that allows your child to give you a simple yes or no answer. Always ask questions that will encourage conversation.

Don't ask:
"Were you at the mall today with Jill?" She will only say yes.

Do ask:
"Who did you go to the mall with?" She will say "Jill, Jenny, Brenda, and Brad." When she says Brad's name, you should give her a physical response that tells her you are surprised she was with Brad. Pause, using the ten-second rule. She will likely begin to tell you more details about how Brad came into the picture.

Don't ask:
"Did Jill steal a t-shirt?" Her answer will depend on how much she trusts you and what your reaction will be.

Do ask:
"Why did Jill steal that t-shirt?" She will initially be surprised at the

question and may even deny knowing what you are talking about, but stick to the ten-second rule and repeat the question. "Why did Jill steal that t-shirt?"

There is no reason to try to get her to admit that Jill stole a t-shirt: after all, you already know this from the conversation you had with Jill's mother. Your goal is not to get your daughter to admit that Jill stole a t-shirt, but to find out if she did as well.

Always offer your child an out

You want to stimulate conversation so that you can prevent future problems and reduce the potential risks that your teenager may be facing. It is not about control, power, proof, and conviction. For parents and children it is about nourishing and encouraging communication and preventing the incident from repeating itself.

If all signs point to the fact that your daughter stole the t-shirt, you already have the evidence you need. Remember you are not the police, and don't need to prove it beyond reasonable doubt. You will know that she did it by the way she talks about the situation, her physical actions, and her discomfort.

Now you need to offer her an out. Do so by saying something like this: "Did you steal a t-shirt too so that Jill would think you were not afraid?" In order for your daughter to answer a question like this, she will have to spend some time explaining herself, which will offer you vital details.

If she only answers no, this could mean that she stole the t-shirt but not for the reason you suggested. Encourage her to explain why.

If she answers yes, you have the proof you need, and now you should focus on dealing with the issue of theft and consequences.

If your daughter admits to stealing a t-shirt, or involvement in any other action that you are concerned about—be it drugs, criminal activity, or simply breaking curfew—you will need to be sure that your reaction is consistent.

Each conversation with your teen is an opportunity to learn more about who she is and where she is headed. There are a lot of influences on teens today, some good, some empowering, some dangerous, and some misleading. It is vital that your positive and supportive influence be the most powerful of them all.

The key to keeping your teen safe is to stay as connected to her as possible. At times this may seem difficult and even impossible, but I promise that if your teen feels confident that you will be there for her no matter what she has done, who she was with, what rules she broke, how she feels, what or who she likes, and what she wants out of her life, she will come to you when it matters most. She will still surprise you, she will still test you, but she will trust your unconditional love. This is what will assist her in making important decisions that can affect her safety when you are not there to do it for her.

Chapter Ten

Techno-Safety: Can Electronic Gizmos Keep Your Kids Safe?

We have hired a nanny to care for our daughter, Melissa, who is eight months old. I have had to return to work earlier than expected, and with my husband's and my schedules, it isn't feasible to take our baby to a day-care. We put an ad in the newspaper and interviewed a lot of different applicants, and though we liked a couple of them, none of them really stood out. We ran out of time and settled on one nanny who is very nice, but I still am not crazy about her. We have been considering putting in a "nanny cam" so that we can watch what she does when we are at work. I am curious about how much time she spends with Melissa. Do nanny cams work?

The only really valuable thing is intuition.

—Albert Einstein

When I was a kid, my mother could reach me by calling through the kitchen window, over the front yard, and across the street into a greenbelt area where my friends and I would play hide and seek. "Jodi!" (my childhood nickname) came in loud and clear every time. She could summon me while elbow-deep in warm, soapy dishwater, her cigarette with its long, perfect ash burning patiently beside her. Of course, in those days, we didn't know that smoking kills, and never imagined that some of the gadgets seen on the Jetsons Saturday morning cartoons were soon to be a reality.

Advancements in technology have made our lives more efficient as they continue to replace labor-intensive daily tasks. Before the arrival of bank machines, it used to take upward of half an hour to stand in a bank lineup to get cash, and scrounging around for a dime to make a phone call was frustrating, to say the least.

But advancements have not just been made to improve our work and play, they are also beginning to make a serious impact on the way parents look at protecting their kids. I am a true supporter of technology and the need for new and more efficient ways of accomplishing important tasks. I am reluctant, however, to transfer the job of protecting kids completely over to the "techies" of the world.

Proactive or Reactive?

When we consider any personal-safety technology, the most important criterion for effectiveness is whether the technology is *proactive* or *reactive*. In my approach to child safety, I always place greater value on technologies—or any other tactic, plan, strategy, or action—that are proactive. Preventing violence is better than reacting to it.

Most products that fall into the category of personal-safety devices are reactive rather than proactive. That is, they respond to or record data about situations that have already gone bad. Unfortunately, many parents are confused about what these products do, usually because they mistakenly believe the claims of those who advertise these products. "Protect your kids," the ads caution. "Get them fingerprinted today!" Or, "Protect your kids: get them a cell phone!" But these are misleading and misguided messages.

If your safety plan focuses only on what you or your child will do in the event of a crisis, your child will be left open to dangers—he may actually need those products! But by the time a reactive-based safety product kicks into gear, it is often too late. The risks are simply too high to rely solely on these types of products.

From this point forward, test whether any personal-safety device you are considering is reactive or proactive. Ask the following question: "Will this product or plan prevent an incident from happening in the first place?"

For example, a personal alarm will not stop someone from

attacking you, though it may draw attention after you have been attacked, and fear of detection and capture may cause your attacker to flee. The personal alarm is, by its nature, reactive.

If you determine that a product is reactive, be aware that it may not protect you or your family. You will need to assess where this product might fit into your safety planning.

I am not suggesting that there is no place for reactive methods. Sometimes, no matter how diligent you are, bad things happen. Reactive methods can make the best of a bad situation. A great example is a fire escape plan, which you will only need if a fire breaks out. By its nature, a fire escape plan is reactive, but it is also essential in keeping your family safe in the event of a fire. The same goes for a fire extinguisher and smoke alarms. These are all essential reactive and responsive products that do not prevent fire but give you the tools to react quickly and safely to reduce the threat. Should these be your only preparations for a fire? No, you should also be using proactive, or preventive, methods of ensuring fire safety, by following a regular schedule of cleaning your furnace filters, checking for gas leaks, and repairing old electrical wiring.

Undeniably, how you respond to danger is a crucial part of keeping your family safe. You've probably heard that the speed with which parents and police react to a problem can make the difference between life and death. And many safety products make useful, even fantastic, investigative tools. They are not without merit—as long as you don't mistake them for being preventive.

When considering personal safety for your children, focus first on proactive, preventive methods. These methods concentrate on the all-important window of time before good turns to bad. Instead of concerning yourself with what happens when the predator is sitting next to your child, consider how he got from the door to the couch in the first place. To being truly proactive in protecting your child, you need to build strong communication with her, add several layers of protection, and watch for the warning signs from those who could potentially harm her. Your goal is to *prevent* your child from becoming a victim.

Personal-Safety Technology: The Good, the Bad, and the Useless

I was a guest on a television talk show that discussed the issue of whether parents were actually becoming too paranoid about their children's safety. One guest was a lovely mother of four youngsters. She was asked to appear on the show because she was a good representative of a caring mother who was very concerned for her children's safety. She and her husband read all the books, watched TV specials, and attempted to absorb anything that might help her in her quest for ultimate protection of her very precious offspring. She truly was a fantastic, loving mom.

Like many great moms, especially those with several young children, she was also very organized. She had brought with her a plastic tub that was her children's ID kit. It contained envelopes clearly marked with each child's name. Inside each envelope was a written record of each child's birthdate, hair and eye color, as well as nail clippings and hair strands for DNA samples, and fingerprints and toothprints (dental imprints). She was happy to show her kit to me, along with the lovely but unsmiling pictures of her children. I was curious as to why the kids seemed so sad. She was quick to explain that the best photo to have of a child for an ID kit was one with the child not smiling. I couldn't help imagining that photo day, when these usually happy children were told not to smile so their pictures could be added to an ID kit.

I was very impressed with this woman and her dedication to her children's safety. Although she claimed not to be overconcerned or paranoid, I feel certain that if a new technique or gadget that claimed to protect her kids were to hit the market, she would be first in line.

She is not alone. It is difficult to ignore the steady stream of child-safety-related products available both online and through traditional retailers. Each product makes its own claim: to control Internet use, prevent abduction, recover lost kids, etc. Ultimately, each promises to put parents' minds at ease. But do these products really protect your kids, and should you entrust your child's life to them?

With technology moving ahead so quickly, there will soon be other products on the market. For now, I've used a star system to rate a number of the most popular technological wonders available at the moment. Zero stars indicate a product that I consider useless; three stars indicate a must-have.

Child identification kits

Child identification kits have been around for many years, and they tend to get renewed attention just after a high-profile child abduction has hit the papers. You will find child identification booths set up at schools, fairs, malls, or anywhere else that children and parents frequent. Many child ID stations are staffed and sponsored by local police or by national child safety organizations such as Child Find Canada.

Just in case you've never heard of a child ID kit, they contain the following:

- A current photograph of the child.
- Fingerprints.
- A DNA sample (either nail clippings or hair strands).
- Dental imprints (also called "toothprints").
- A record of the child's particulars (height/weight/hair color/marks or scars).
- Emergency information (allergies or other medical concerns).

A child ID kit is promoted in two ways. In the past, and even now, I hear marketing messages like this: "Prevent child abduction. Have a child ID kit for each child." More recently, however, the message has changed to this: "Help recover your child quickly."

Although the latter statement is more accurate, it is still misleading. Fingerprints and child ID kits do not help *find* children. They can be an investigative tool, but there is no need to yank a strand of hair from your child's head, save fingernail clippings, or swab their mouths. The police will be able to collect your child's DNA and fingerprints easily from almost any area of your home. But heaven forbid they should have to.

Police are likely to use fingerprints and DNA samples to help identify a recovered child in the following circumstances.

- If the child's appearance has changed dramatically from the time he or she went missing (usually if a lengthy period of time has passed).
- To identify a deceased child.
- To determine if any evidence the police have is related to the abduction case.

There is one valuable part of a child ID kit: a recent photograph of your child. This, by the way, should be kept with you when you are out with your kids. If your child goes missing in a mall, that photograph will be tremendously useful in helping others search for and effectively identify him. If the photograph is sitting in a kit, tucked away in your closet at home, you will be wasting valuable time.

I find child ID kits most useful as vehicles to create an opportunity to talk about personal safety with your child. You can sit together and fill out the information cards, take photographs, and assemble the kit with him while discussing how to be a safe kid. Then put it away. You will likely never use it. Of course, child ID kits can't hurt, as long as you understand that they cannot prevent your child from going missing. **One star.**

Child personal safety alarms

Child personal alarms are abundant on the market. They perform the same way as an adult personal alarm, key alarm, or any other device that is designed to make a loud screeching noise, thereby alerting passersby that you are in trouble. They are sold with the promise that they will keep your child safe.

Designed to be small enough to fit into children's hands, these mini-alarms can also be clipped to belt loops, backpacks—anything that the child wears or carries. The alarm is fitted with a release pin or a panic button: if the child feels threatened and needs help, she is instructed to sound the alarm, and that help will come running. But what if no one is around to hear it? What if no one pays attention to it? After all, we have all grown quite accustomed to the sound of car alarms these days, and few of us give them more than a second's notice. There are obvious concerns with claiming that a loud siren will keep your kids safe.

What is dangerous is that personal alarm systems often give a false sense of security to those who use them. Children especially can fall into the trap of feeling safe, and therefore put themselves in risky situations that they might not otherwise have attempted. Personal alarms are very loud, and they may draw attention, but they are entirely reactive—and they will not protect your child. **Zero stars.**

Bullet-proof and knife-proof clothing

What a horrifying thought: to live in a community where children face such life-threatening dangers as stray bullets, knife attacks, and gang violence that parents are resorting to dressing their children in protective gear.

This is not as far-out as you may think. In some neighborhoods in the United States, children are wearing bullet-proof jackets as they walk to school through gang-infested areas. It is not that children are being shot at, but drive-by shootings and random acts of violence are so prevalent that kids are at risk.

I am proud to say that in Canada we have not seen such dire circumstances—yet. However, these items, which are usually reserved for police and military, are being manufactured to fit children. Regular items of clothing, including sweatshirts, coats, and vests, are being made knife-resistant and bullet-proof.

Are these items proactive, and will they protect your child? Yes and no. Kevlar is a product that can deflect a direct knife puncture, but it does not prevent wounds from slashing. Depending on the type of gun, bullet, and distance from the victim, as well as the angle and location of the shot, a bullet-proof vest may prevent the bullet from penetrating, injuring, and killing. When I was a cop, I wore a bullet-proof vest with a trauma plate under my uniform. It gave me a sense of comfort, but not entirely. Even though wearing a bullet-proof vest reduced the risk of fatal injury from a stab or gunshot wound to the chest or back, I was still vulnerable everywhere else on my body.

It will be a true failure in our society if parents are driven to cloaking their children in Kevlar to get them to school safely. **Zero stars, for now.**

Child identification scopes

Child ID scopes are products designed to hold vital information about your child in case they are lost, or in an accident and need medical attention. You might think of them as a combination of a child ID kit and a medical alert bracelet. They are small pieces of jewelry, about the size of a five-cent coin, which children wear either as a pendant on a necklace or as a bracelet. If you look through the end of the scope, you can see the child's vital information, including name, address, phone number, where the parents can be reached and, most important, any vital medical information such as disease, allergies, or other conditions.

These scopes are not marketed as a way to protect your child, but rather as method to ensure that vital information is received by the right people in the case of an emergency if you are not close by. One drawback is that child ID scopes are not as obvious as medical alert bracelets, and they may go unnoticed and unused. However, if your child has a medical condition, I recommend looking into this creative new way to store and retrieve vital information (www.escopes.com). **Two stars.**

Internet monitoring software

There is little doubt that the Internet has opened the world to kids. It's a world that includes some images and text that are inappropriate for children. Internet safety is forefront in the minds of parents, educators, child safety advocates, and technology-based entrepreneurs.

Most ISPs (Internet service providers) have parental controls and monitoring systems in place that can assist parents in their quest to limit access to questionable content on the Net. A plethora of filtering programs—too many to mention—is also available.

But it's important for parents to understand that monitoring and filtering software have limits. The first is that Internet-savvy kids can easily disable most programs and allow the restricted content in. Remember, kids are usually more computer literate than their parents, and a disabled program can easily go unnoticed. The second limit of the software is that many programs fail to block upward of 20 percent of inappropriate sites, not to mention the fact that sometimes the parameters you designate will block some good and useful sites.

There are other ways of finding out if your child is accessing questionable or dangerous Internet content. Built into any web browser (Internet Explorer or Netscape, for instance) is a history of sites visited. Files are usually kept for a period of time in the history folder. The key can be found at the top toolbar of most versions of Internet Explorer (click on View, then choose Explorer Bar and then choose History), or try hitting the Control (Ctrl) key + H at the same time. This will give you a listing of the most recent sites visited.

Filtering tools can help parents, but the best way to be sure your child is safe online is through parental supervision and open communication. You should have some sort of filtering software or program if your children are online; however, these will not replace direct supervision, nor will they block everything. **Three stars.**

Internet remote control systems

Now here is a system that is new and interesting, a system that falls somewhere between a preventive and reactive measure. There is a new program developed by a company in the United States called Sentry Remote (www.searchhelp.com). This company has devised a version of monitoring software that goes one step further than most. For a monthly or yearly subscription fee (around US$8 per month) parents can stay connected to their kids, via their children's computers, from just about anywhere.

Here is how it works. Parents download the software onto the computer their child uses. Parents can set guidelines, key words, or catch phrases that will trigger an alert to be sent to the parent's cell phone or e-mail box, in real time. For example, if the child is instant messaging on MSN messenger, and a catchphrase like "don't tell your parents" is typed into the chat, a parent will instantly receive an e-mail or text message that tells them this has just occurred.

If the parent is able to receive this message, and has access to the Internet, he can log on to the system and view the conversation in six-second snapshots. From there, the parent can redirect the computer, or ultimately shut it down from wherever he is at the time.

There are some technical issues that need to be considered before investing in such a program.

- It works only if it is loaded onto the computer the child is using. You will not be able to monitor other computers that your child has access to, such as those in public Internet cafés.
- It operates (at this time) only on a select number of operating systems, which may not be the operating system you have on your child's computer.
- Children will know that you have the software installed and therefore there is a risk that they will disable it.
- Parents need to have access to the Internet when an alert is received.
- This system does not replace direct parental supervision.

Aside from the technical issues, you will also need to consider whether the breach of trust and privacy inherent in such a system is worth the added security. You will have to determine if your wish to use such a system stems from your own curiosity or from a belief that it is necessary to ensure proper supervision of your children while online.

If you choose to use this system, be sure to explain the benefits to your children before installing it. Help them understand that it is not them that you do not trust, but that you are watching for anything a predator might do in approaching them. You are not trying to pry into their personal lives but want to ensure that a predator has minimal chance of gaining access to them. If you discuss your concerns and motives to your children clearly, and they understand that you will tell them each time you use the software to gain more information, they may trust your motives and actually feel safer knowing that you are still watching out for them when you can't be there in person.

This system is unique and has some clear benefits, largely because it helps parents to supervise their children's online activities, something that becomes more difficult as children grow older and more independent. Because it is designed to respond and alert almost instantly (within six seconds of the infraction), parents can quickly intercept and end an inappropriate conversation or image. At the time of writing this book, Sentry Remote had been available for only two months, and had obviously not been rigorously tested by the marketplace. However, if you are concerned that your child is breaking online safety rules when you are not present, Sentry Remote may be worth looking into. **Two stars.**

Nanny cams
In policing, an "agent" is someone who is used to trick a criminal into committing an illegal act. Working for or on behalf of police, the agent willingly and knowingly puts himself in a position that might allow police to record the criminal doing something wrong. When you place hidden cameras in strategic locations throughout your home, with the intention of catching your child's caregiver in the act of neglecting or otherwise abusing your child, you are unwittingly making an agent of your child.

Putting a child in the role of an agent—for any reason—is very dangerous, not to mention barbaric. Hidden surveillance cameras (nanny cams) are completely reactive: they will do nothing to prevent your child from being abused. If you suspect that your child is being abused or neglected by her caregiver, do not allow that nanny into your home or to be with your child one moment more.

As a parent, you already have a nanny cam built into your being. It is called intuition and it is as accurate as a video recording, except it is preventive rather than reactive. If you have felt the urge to install a hidden camera in your home to watch how your nanny cares for your kids, you must have already been picking up intuitive signals that something might be up. There was something in the way she responded to your questions, something changing in your children, some other clues that led you to think that you now need proof. You don't need proof—you already have it. Your intuition is all the proof you need. Trust it and end the relationship there.

Nanny cams are a thriving business, and once again the marketing of these products preys on fear and guilt that many parents experience when having to select a caregiver for their kids. Is this person safe? Will she abuse my child? Can I trust her? These are all valid questions that you must answer without reservation before a caregiver spends one moment with your child. They are not questions you should be exploring after the fact.

Hidden cameras are offered by spy companies or online. They can be tiny and hidden in almost anything. Some are sold as complete kits, while other companies offer a rental program, mostly because they know that the camera will be used for only a short period of time: either the parents will tire of watching hours and hours of tape with nothing on it, or the nanny will be caught in the act.

Cameras are also used by parents if they suspect that the nanny may be stealing from them. Video evidence will provide proof of the offense, but there are legal issues surrounding your right to videotape a person in the first place. It's also important to realize that you don't need concrete evidence of a theft before you dismiss the nanny or anyone else in your employment. There is something called "exclusive opportunity" in proving theft cases. Although eyewitnesses provide the most foolproof evidence, if you can prove that an individual had exclusive opportunity to steal an item, you are likely to prove the theft.

When you consider the safety of your child, you'll see why you should not wait to act on your intuition. If you believe there is even a possibility that your caregiver may be abusing your child, do not put your child in potential danger again. Simply dismiss your caregiver at once. **Zero stars.**

Global Positioning Systems (GPS)

The GPS is a multi-billion-dollar satellite system that was developed by the U.S. Department of Defense for the military. It is a network of satellites that was sent into orbit, and since the 1980s the system has been free for public use. The navigation system can track and locate a subject at any time, anywhere, regardless of whether the subject is moving or not. GPS works in any weather and any conditions, and is accurate within fifteen meters.

If a child is lost or abducted, time is the most valuable commodity in the success of recovering him safe and alive. Studies show that over 90 percent of non-parental child abduction victims are killed within the first twenty-four hours. However, without assistance, locating an abducted child, with no initial suspect, is like finding the proverbial needle in a haystack.

Innovative engineers who understood the speed and accuracy and availability of GPS decided to adopt the technology to assist in locating lost or abducted children. They have come up with a variety of products, some better than others.

Wristwatch GPS

A company called Wherify Wireless (www.wherifywireless.com) has designed a personal locator for kids in the form of a wristwatch. It is a GPS system that helps parents to locate, track, and communicate with their children. They do all of this through a heavy wristwatch that has both GPS and wireless radio.

The child can even receive pages and hit a panic button if he or she is in need of immediate assistance, which will call 911. If you have access to the Web, you can log on and search for your child, or simply use a telephone to call the service and have it track your child for you. If your child is wearing the wristwatch, this technology will allow you to locate her within several feet in about a minute.

When I heard about this product, my first concern was that the child could take the watch off, or it could be broken off (accidentally or by a predator). Parents would then be successful in locating only the watch, not the child. However, I learned that the watch has been "kid tested" and is durable, waterproof, slash-proof, and has a safety lock and key fob that help prevent it from being removed.

The more important question is, Will this product prevent my child from going missing? The answer is no. Another question: If my child is missing, will this product help me find her faster? Likely yes—as long as she is still wearing the watch.

The technology is quite expensive: monthly service plans currently range from $US19.95 to $US44.05. Most parents will not budget for the expense of a reactive device. Too bad it is so expensive, since it has merit. **One and a half stars.**

GPS phone systems

GPS technology can be placed in a cell phone rather than a wristwatch. Let's face it: most kids, and almost all teenagers, have cell phones. Parents are being sold on the idea of the cell-phone GPS because they are told they will be able to find their teenagers anywhere by subscribing. The problem is this: although cell phones are well guarded by most kids, what happens if your child forgets his phone at home, lends it to a friend, drops it, breaks it, or otherwise loses it? You will only be successful in locating the phone, not necessarily the teenager. **Half a star only because it is not totally useless.**

Identification chip implants (a.k.a. Verichip)

In 2002, a family (mother, father, and son) from Baton Rouge, Florida, volunteered to be the first family to receive a medical Verichip ID implant under their skin. The mother was also a shareholder for Applied Digital Solutions, a company that has since been approved to market the Verichip implant. The chip is about the size of a grain of rice, and it is inserted under the skin. The entire procedure takes about twenty minutes and does not require stitches.

However, there is a catch. At the time of writing, the chip can only be used for medical purposes, such as identifying Alzheimer patients or giving other patient-specific information. The information is conveyed through a bar code, much like a UPC code on food items at the grocery store.

The Verichip does have the potential to one day incorporate GPS technology. This would mean that, as with a permanent GPS wristwatch, the child's exact location could be determined in case of emergency. Of course, this technology has a way to go before it will be useful as a child-finding tool, and even when perfected it will remain only a reactive safety measure. As well, it raises some valid and controversial concerns about relinquishing privacy. **Zero stars, for now.**

Vehicle GPS and monitoring software

As a parent of a teenager who is new to driving, I found that this product made me sit up and take notice. There is a company in the United States called Alltrack USA (www.alltrackusa.com) that has designed technology to track and monitor your vehicle while your teenager is driving it.

Similar to a system used by police to reduce auto theft (bait cars), Alltrack uses GPS and monitoring software to help you find out how fast your teenager is driving, how far she is driving, and where she went. You can essentially monitor your teenager's driving habits from any computer. With access to the Internet, you can even lock the car doors, disable the starter, or turn the lights on or off. You can receive alerts that your car is being driven over a set speed limit, or has crossed into a part of town that you have prohibited your teenager to enter.

Essentially, you can watch and record her every move—or at least the vehicle's every move. This definitely brings up the issue of your teenager's right to privacy. The argument, however, is that driving is a privilege in Canada, not a fundamental right. Permitting your child to drive your car is also a privilege.

Will this product prevent your teenager from getting in an accident? Likely not. However, will it prevent him from speeding? Maybe. That would depend on the consequences you put in place as a parent for breaking the rules.

The price of this product is currently $US425 plus monthly fees ranging from $8.50 to $66 depending on usage.

The Alltrack system provides an innovative and creative way to keep track of your teenagers, and to monitor them when you can't. It is still a reactive method, but not entirely useless. If you can afford it, it's worth considering. **One star.**

Child perimeter alarms

Claiming to "protect children from abduction, child predators, and drowning," inventors have come up with an alarm system that alerts parents if their child has gone outside preset boundaries. The alarm system is very similar to a wireless dog fence, except we are talking about children.

Here's how it works. Parents fix an alarm to the child's clothing and set the perimeter to the receiver. If a child wanders outside these boundaries, the alarm on the receiver will sound. This system is fiercely marketed as a way to "save your child's life." Hogwash. You can save your child's life and prevent her from drowning or abduction by supervising her with your eyes, not by using a remote device that costs upward of $200.

That said, these alarm systems are excellent as an *added* layer of protection around a swimming pool where you already have a fence, locked gate, doors, and other safety assurances. The alarm is the last resort, not the first line of defense. **One star.**

Cell phones/camera phones

Cell phones have become a staple in today's society not only for business people but also to keep families and friends connected.

The wireless technology industry is a multi-billion-dollar industry designed to attract new customers and develop new products and services before the competition. For the most part, it is quite exciting to see what they will think of next.

Parents often insist on their kids having cell phones. They know the benefits of being able to reach their kids at any time. Teenagers rarely turn their phones off, so the chances of reaching them are pretty good. Parents also believe that their children are safer when carrying cell phones because they can always call for help if needed. True, for the most part, but not completely foolproof.

Cell phones are a communication tool, not a protective device. They will assist you and your child in calling for help if he is lost or stranded in a vehicle; they will allow you to report a crime, accident, or any other emergency situation. But just because your child has the technology to call for help does not mean he will have the ability to do so. Many girls carry their phones in their purses; if a girl is grabbed from behind, the cell phone at the bottom of her purse will be useless to her.

Cell phones keep you in touch, but they do not prevent crimes. What you may not know, however, is that all cell phones, once activated, have 911 capability, regardless of whether the phone plan has been deactivated. All cell phone customers pay into the 911 service and it is always active. Any old cell phone will call 911 if needed.

Cell phones have become a staple in today's society. I recommend them for their convenience and affordability, but stress caution in relying on them entirely as a proactive means of keeping your kids safe. **Three stars.**

Where Do We Go from Here?

Technology will continue to advance, with new products and services constantly being launched that will claim to eliminate crimes and harm to children. Some companies will just be out to get your money, but others will come up with solid, useful products that will increase your family's safety. It will be up to you to decide whether a product is proactive or reactive, and whether you will give it a place in your family's safety plan.

It is okay to be concerned for your child's safety. I have dedicated my life and career to the pursuit of keeping kids safe. I believe it is possible to protect children without paranoia. Though not technologically sophisticated, keeping open lines of communication, understanding threats and warning signs, and exercising common sense and good judgment are still the best ways to keep your kids safe.

Conclusion

Rules for Safe Families to Live By

About the time that I finished writing this book, I heard the news of a disaster that literally rocked the world. We were all shocked and saddened by the tens of thousands who lost their lives or livelihoods in the tsunami that struck Southeast Asia on December 26, 2004. Those lives will be forever mourned.

Even though scientists seek to understand the earth better and make it safer for all of us, the earth and its elements are still largely beyond our control. The unfortunate truth is that natural disasters are a fact of life. There is often little we can do to prevent them; we can only prepare as best we know how, then hope for the best.

Many parents think of their child's safety in similar terms: "Let's keep our fingers crossed that it doesn't happen to us!"

Child safety disasters, however, are not the same as natural disasters. You have much more control over the elements that your children face. You have the power to determine who comes into their lives. You choose how high you will allow them to climb the monkey bars, how long they can stay out at night with friends, and you set rules that will help keep them safe when they are left to make decisions on their own. Crimes and violence against kids are not unavoidable natural occurrences. *They are preventable.*

You can teach yourself, and prepare your family, to react safely to an emergency; in fact, both of these are important factors in safety education. But your goal in achieving a safe family will be to avoid having to react in the first place. In everything that your family does, and with each person who comes into contact with you and your children, think first about preventive and proactive approaches to your safety. Train your brain to assess people, places, and situations quickly and accurately.

Here are some tips that you can apply to your everyday life to help you achieve your goals.

1. Listen to your instincts. Question everything. You have a natural ability to sense danger. If your instinct is telling you there is danger, there is—period.

2. Anticipate worst-case scenarios through role-play. Prepare for the unexpected by role-playing potential dangers, making sure your scenarios are realistic. Know the difference between real and perceived danger and how to react.

3. Lead with your eyes and mind. Look ahead and beyond what is in front of you. Know your surroundings before you pass them. Think about clues that are presented to you and try to understand their meanings.

4. Don't jump recklessly into unsafe situations. Although television shows like to make you believe that cops act on the spur of the moment, they simply don't. Neither should you. That would be stupid, dangerous, and even deadly.

When cops take action, they are assessing each person, place, and event—sometimes at lightning speed—for its threat level and risk factor. Surveillance, assessment, and planning are what make it possible for cops to return to their families at the end of the day—not complacency, recklessness, or fearlessness.

Although I am certain that you, a parent, would throw yourself into danger to protect your children, you don't need to. You just have to recognize when it's a good time to run in the other direction.

5. Always call for help. You are never alone. More people will help you than hurt you—believe that. Don't be afraid to ask for help—

you are not bothering anyone. Recognize your limitations. Don't go into a dangerous place or situation, alone or with others, if your instincts tell you otherwise.

6. Resist complacency. Complacency is the number-one reason for victimization. Don't wait until tomorrow to fix the locks on your doors, and never believe that it can't happen to you. Anything is possible—and everyone is equal when it comes to dangers.

7. Get involved. It takes a community to keep kids safe. Learn about what dangers are specific to your community. Attend town meetings, express your opinions, and speak up for kids and their safety. Spend time at your child's school. Get to know the principal, teachers, and students. Question anything you are unsure of.

Overcome any unwillingness you may have about reporting a crime to the police. Do it anonymously if you like, but always—always—report any suspicious activity or people to the police. Simply by being a member of your community, you are already involved, and the information you give—no matter how insignificant it may seem—could be a turning point in an investigation. It could ultimately save a life or result in getting a creep off the streets where your children play.

Most criminals are caught because the police received tips from people just like you. The police can't be everywhere and they need your help. Consider the success of at least 789 criminal captures resulting from the popularity of the TV show *America's Most Wanted*. These captures happened because people got involved.

8. Trust yourself and your ability to protect your family. The truth of the matter is that if you have picked up this book, and are now here, at the conclusion, you are already committed to keeping your family safe. Commitment, perseverance, and intolerance for anything less than the best for your kids are essential traits in a safe parent.

Don't be fooled into thinking that your children can protect themselves before they are ready. They are only the very first layer of protection—you are the last and most important one. Hang on to your children until it is safe to let go.

The Internet has opened the world to your kids, and technology pushes us eagerly into seeking new ways to protect them. But in fact you already have the most powerful tools right at your fingertips. Keeping the lines of communication open and committing yourself to proper supervision of your children are the keys to their safety. There is no magic gadget, trick, cloak, or weapon that will ultimately keep your kids safe. Safe families are dedicated *as a family* to staying safe.

Disasters happen; in our world, that is a constant. But another constant is that safe kids have safe families. It *is* that simple—because crimes can be prevented, violence is predictable, and knowledge is the key.

Acknowledgments

Thank you to Iris Tupholme and Kevin Hanson, for believing in my message and providing the venue to present it. Thanks to the entire team at HarperCollins Canada for your dedication to the success of this project.

Special thanks to Nicole Langlois. You are such an incredible talent and have undoubtedly made me far more eloquent than I really am. You have been a great support throughout this project, always keeping me on the right track and bringing out the best in my abilities. Thank you again.

Thanks to my agents, Dean Cooke, Suzanne Brandreth, and Samantha North, whom I came to rather by fluke. I think this must be the only time that something fantastic came of having the flu! Thank you, Dean, for your professionalism, insight, and direction. I value you and your opinions tremendously.

Thanks to all my staff at Kidproof Canada, and to every instructor. Your dedication to me, and to my mission of keeping all kids safe, is undeniable. I am forever grateful.

Thank you to every police officer I had the pleasure of working with over the years, especially those who took me under their wing as a rookie and taught me more about communication and living than I could ever have hoped for. I am blessed to have known you all, and am a better person for it.

Thank you to my family:

To my mother and friend, Brenda Elvins, without whose encouragement, support, and unconditional love I would never have succeeded. Words cannot express how grateful I am to have you.

Acknowledgments

To my sister, Tammy, for always finding a way to make me laugh.

To my husband, Terry, for being my biggest fan. I have to pinch myself to make sure I am not dreaming.

Finally, thank you to my boys, London and Conrad. You are my reason for living and for all that I do. Love, Mom.

Index

Index